CONTENTS

ABOUT THE AUTHOR

Charles Gardner is a 63-year-old Cape Town-born journalist who has worked in the newspaper industry for 40 years. Part-Jewish, he grew up in South Africa and became a fully committed Christian as a young man living in London before moving to Yorkshire more than 33 years ago. He is currently working on plans to launch a new UK national newspaper reporting and interpreting the news from a biblical perspective. With four children and seven grandchildren, he is married to Linda, 55, who takes the Christian message around dozens of schools in the large northern town of Doncaster.

ACKNOWLEDGEMENTS

This book is dedicated to the late Alan Brooke who taught me so much about Israel, deepening my understanding of the issues involved and especially how the Scriptures relate to them. Alan lived in Israel with his family for a number of years after offering his services to the fledgling nation as a dentist. With his lovely wife Daphne, he led a Prayer For Israel group in Doncaster for seven years before he died suddenly in October 2011, aged 82.

I have also been indebted over the years for their perception of this complicated political and religious subject to Dr Clifford Hill, Nick Thompson, Rev Niall Griffin and many more, some of whom are quoted in these pages.

Special thanks are due to Trevor and Margaret Davies for their invaluable help and encouragement. And I would also like to dedicate the book to the welfare and well-being of Jewish people everywhere – the chief purpose for which it was written.

FOREWORD

This is a significant book in that it takes a topic at the centre of God's Word that has been pushed to the periphery by a Western church eager to be socially acceptable – even at the price of becoming unacceptable to God.

The established church has over many centuries worked assiduously at severing its links to our Hebraic heritage. In doing so they have removed much of the original meaning from our Bibles as well as depriving us of the words and terms Jesus used to cross-reference Original Testament content. Perhaps most significant is the change in understanding as to the meaning of righteousness. We have changed a meaning of acts of covenant faithfulness to one of judicial legitimacy.

This book challenges that thinking and flags up three key issues that I believe to be fundamental to determining the state of our relationship with God:

1. The need to be God-centred: Everything Jesus did was focused on God, or theocentric in academic language. Sadly our modern world is far too often egocentric – How do I get my act together?

2. Life before death: Far too often our focus is on going to glory when in actual fact we are here as witnesses to the glory of God. Getting a right perspective on our Hebraic heritage helps us focus on being good witnesses.

3. The centrality of Israel in God's plans. The Bible tells us that Jesus will return as the Lion of Judah – and not to London, Rome, New York or Beijing, but to Jerusalem! The fulfilment of prophecy that has seen Israel's restoration in living memory is I believe a precursor to this. If you want to get a true perspective on your relationship with God, then you have to accept that Israel is God's chosen. As Jeremiah 31: 35-37 puts it: "This is what Adonai says, who gives the sun as light for the day, who ordained the laws for the moon and stars to provide the light for the night, who stirs up the sea until its waves roar – Adonai Tzva'ot (The Lord of Hosts) is his name. If these laws leave my presence, says Adonai, then the offspring of Israel will stop being a nation in my pres-

ence forever." This is what Adonai says: "If the sky can be measured and the foundations of the earth be fathomed, then I will reject all the offspring of Israel for all that they have done, says Adonai."

I commend this book to you, but most of all I commend the God of Israel, Abraham and Isaac.

– NICK THOMPSON
Friend and colleague, Methodist lay preacher, scholar of Christianity's Hebraic roots and managing director of Hull City Football Club.

INTRODUCTION

Part I: Apocalypse Now

Frightening apocalyptic events have shocked and terrified us in recent days. I think of the awesome Boxing Day tsunami that devastated much of South-East Asia in 2004 and the more recent one that struck Japan in the wake of a huge earthquake with 'quakes also causing massive damage in New Zealand and elsewhere. And who can forget the terrorist attacks on the Twin Towers of New York more than a decade ago when millions around the world watched in horror on TV as 110-storey buildings deliberately struck by jet aircraft hijacked by suicide bombers came crashing to earth in one unbelievable movement, leaving a heap of rubble and thousands dead. I have since discovered that such an attack was originally the concept of Adolf Hitler, who apparently delighted at the prospect of sending light aircraft packed with explosives crashing into the skyscrapers of New York – home to two million Jews!

Coinciding with these natural disasters and terrorist attacks, which have been growing apace both in frequency and severity, are political upheavals across the world – especially in Muslim nations and particularly in the Middle East. The word 'apocalypse' is used to describe events of 'biblical' proportions such as the prophecies recorded in the Book of Revelation (the last book of the Bible) and foretold by Jesus himself, the fulfilment of which would see disaster on a scale you might until now only have seen at the movies.

And the climax of it all would be played out on a gigantic battlefield known as Armageddon (a huge plain in Israel) which would be far worse, and more real, than any disaster movie you have seen but which would also – ironically, following the use of ferocious weapons leading to a possible nuclear holocaust – usher in a time of unprecedented peace and prosperity.

In the eye of the storm is Israel, harassed and persecuted throughout the ages and now bombarded from all sides by a conglomerate of nations determined to wipe her off the map. But, oh, the injustice of it all... Why does a nation representing less than half of one per cent of the world's population, and taking up only a tiny proportion of its rightful territory, attract so much hatred and vilification while the vicious acts of her enemies are largely ignored? Why is a nation that has provided some of the most brilliant minds of the modern world despised and rejected? Why are they the focus of media attention in these 'apocalyptic' days when there is so much wrong elsewhere? Politicians and others will offer many simplistic answers, and some so-called 'Christians' will explain that it is because the Jews rejected Jesus. But none of these theories is anywhere near the mark and there is so much ignorance on the subject – in Parliament, council chambers and in church pews – which is why I have written this book.

The apology given by the authors of the London Olympics website for listing Israel as being in Europe and Palestine – a state not yet even officially formed – as in Asia with its capital Jerusalem, blamed "incorrect data input" which neatly sums up the modern world's misconception about the Middle East problem.

The fact is that Israel represents God's chosen people, whether we like it or not, and there is just so much jealousy over that truth. It's dressed up in all sorts of high-sounding, politically-correct language which has led the world's media to soak it up like a sponge. But at the end of the day it's all about a refusal to recognise what God has chosen. If you were God, and you had chosen a bride for yourself, would you not regard it as preposterous if members of your own creation rose up in protest at your choice?

At the heart of it all lies the question put by Satan at the beginning of time, as recorded in the opening book of the Bible: "Did God really say?" The never-changing, totally reliable, Word of God, is being challenged again and again, and the result is an ongoing battle for truth against falsehood.

This book was birthed during a wonderful week's holiday I spent with my wife on the Yorkshire coast – near our favourite spot, Robin Hood's Bay. It was during a rainy day when we stayed inside to read that I felt God clearly speaking to me through various passages from the Book of Isaiah – specifically that he was asking me to be a 'helper of Israel' which is how the Lord describes himself. I had been seeking to do this for some years through involvement (as worship leader) with a Prayer for Israel group and through numerous articles I had written on the subject. But it was some months before I realised he wanted me to write a book, and this is the result. My aim is to produce as clear and concise an explanation as possible of Israel's position and why everyone needs to know this, because it may surprise you to know that we will all be judged by our response to her plight. And my further aim is to challenge and inspire readers to focus on this most important of issues at the centre of which is the Jewish Messiah himself – Yeshua, known to most Westerners as Jesus.

Part II: Bin Laden and the Three Davids

Al Qaeda leader Osama Bin Laden conducted a reign of terror around the world for nearly two decades before he was finally tracked down and killed by American Special Forces. And the man who held the world in fear for so long was motivated almost exclusively by a ferocious hatred of Israel – and all who were perceived to have supported her. The 9/11 attack on New York's 110-storey twin towers was thus essentially an attack on the Jews – harassed, harangued and hated for millennia for reasons it is hard to explain or understand apart from jealousy of a people clearly head and shoulders above others in terms of skill, intellect, natural and spiritual blessings and yet occupying only a tiny proportion of the earth's surface.

And yet what is even more difficult to grasp is that the man described as "pure evil" (a contradiction in itself) also represents the aspirations of millions of Arabs aligned with fundamentalist Islam in plotting the destruction of little, beleaguered Israel – perversely seen as the bully rather than the victim of so much antagonism that its people live in constant fear of rocket attacks and suicide bombers. And this portrayal of the Jewish homeland is mirrored by much of the world's media which, for example, will remain quiet on the subject during a prolonged period of firing on Israeli civilian populations from Gaza until the Israeli Defence Force finally lose patience and strike back with force, so often described by Western politicians as an 'over-reaction'.

The truth is that Israel is no more the bully than was the young David in his confrontation with the Philistine giant Goliath. And it is this sort of bias fed by misleading information, half-truths and downright lies that drives the anti-Semitic agenda. In this high-tech media age where news is transmitted across the world almost instantaneously (often without waiting for the other side of the story) and is accessible by so many means to billions of people, its influence for good or evil is literally explosive. And with the amount of inflammatory material about Israel circulating on the internet and elsewhere, it isn't too surprising that we are being held to ransom by terrorist fanatics.

It is worth noting that at the same time as the monster who ordered the attacks on New York was finally cornered, an extraordinary man who brought the love of the Jewish Messiah, Jesus, to the streets of that same city suffered a violent death in a car crash. His name was David Wilkerson, pastor of New York's Times Square Church who also founded a hugely influential international outreach called Teen Challenge following the success of his mission to bring joy and purpose to the miserable lives of gangsters and drug addicts in that city. The contrast between the two is indeed a matter of "life and death". As the Jewish patriarch Joshua challenged the Israelites so long ago, we too are faced with that choice. Will we recognise God's purposes for his chosen people, or will we too be taken in by the propaganda battle for our minds as we jump into the raging tide seeking to engulf us with humanistic claptrap in a war for the supremacy of our intellects?

Just days after Bin Laden was shot, the verdict was announced following the long-running inquest into the 52 people who died in the 7/7 suicide bombings of London's transport system – yet another atrocity carried out on the orders of the Al Qaeda chief. Among the victims was another brave David, my younger brother, who lost his leg in the Edgware Road tube station blast. He only survived through the courageous acts of others who came to his aid, and through much prayer from around the world I might add, but he was soon back on his 'feet' facing a cruel world with gratitude, determination and complete lack of bitterness – even for the perpetrators.

The horrors of 7/7 are still etched on the memory of all our family – the day terrorism came knocking at our door, reminding us of the plight of the Israelis and others who suffer similar threats on a constant basis. I urge you to follow the three Davids I have mentioned. One man with God is more than a match for a thousand terrorists.

CHAPTER 1

It's time to help Israel!

Have you ever wondered why Jewish people always seem to come out on top, no matter what circumstances of life are thrown at them? I think of celebrity chef Nigella Lawson, featured on BBC Television's 'Who Do You Think You Are?' series. In exploring her family roots, she discovered that her ancestors had fled persecution in Europe to experience poverty in London's East End before rising out of oblivion to head up the giant Lyon's Tetley Tea Company. Then there was Jack Cohen, an East End barrow boy who rose to head up the Tesco supermarket empire. And there's Marks & Spencer, and so much more.

The influence and impact of the Jews on the world is way out of proportion to their numbers. Hitler tried to wipe them out, mercilessly slaughtering six million of them in the most inhumane way possible, but they rose from the ashes to rebuild a nation dispersed from their homeland for nearly 2,000 years. Now again they are under great threat, with surrounding Arab nations wishing to destroy them. And yet their survival against attacks launched against them specifically in 1948, 1967 and 1973 was nothing short of miraculous. Then there is the extraordinary restoration of the Hebrew language 1,200 years after it had faded from everyday use.

This is because they are God's chosen people – the 'apple of his eye'. (Zechariah 2.8) Those who recognise this and act accordingly stand to be richly rewarded, for God promised to bless the nations through Abraham's seed. Those who bless the Jews would themselves be blessed, but those who curse them would invite judgment on themselves.

For centuries leading British evangelicals had predicted the return of the Jews to their ancient homeland in fulfilment of the Scriptures and called on Christians to help their cause and pray for them. Among them were John Wesley, Charles Spurgeon, William Wilberforce, Lord Shaftesbury, Hudson

Taylor and Bishop J C Ryle of Liverpool.

And so, finally, the British Government promised to work for the establishment of such a homeland through the so-called Balfour Declaration in 1917 and, with the defeat in the Holy Land of the Turks by General Allenby's forces that same year, the gates were opened wide for Israel's re-birth and the League of Nations gave Britain the Mandate to oversee such an outcome.

But in its efforts to appease the Arab nations, Britain did not sufficiently honour her pledge or legal obligations. She acted against Jewish interests and blocked Jewish immigration, thus contributing to the deaths of countless Jews who could otherwise have escaped Hitler's 'final solution'.

And she has paid a heavy price, for she has since lost her empire and things are getting worse. The Word of God says of Israel: "For the nation or kingdom that will not serve you will perish; it will be utterly ruined." (Isaiah 60.12)

Former British Prime Minister Tony Blair, to his great credit, refused to criticise Israel for attacking the Hezbollah terrorists in 2006 but, in doing so, was swimming against the tide of popular opinion. He risked support for his leadership, but even greater danger lies in the swirling waters of political correctness over Israel.

Jews have lived in the Promised Land since ancient times but, following their rejection (as a nation) of their Messiah, Jerusalem was destroyed and they were scattered to the four corners of the earth. However, though he has punished them, God has not rejected them. For even before the great dispersion, God had promised that there would come a day when they would be re-gathered to the land of their fathers – from the north, south, east and west. "I will surely save you out of a distant place, your descendants from the land of their exile," is just one example. (Jeremiah 30.10) And another: "See, I will bring them from the land of the north and gather them from the ends of the earth." (Jer 31.8) Many other Old Testament prophecies clearly allude to this great event, which we have seen unfold before our eyes in this generation. Following the holocaust, a newly sympathetic world made room for a Jewish homeland and a barren landscape became settled once more, although some including the British betrayed the Jews by going back on boundary promises – so that the land now occupied by Israel is only a fraction of what the nations had originally agreed. And even then they are prepared to give up more land as the price for peace.

Meanwhile the world clamours for so-called 'Palestinians' to be granted their own land despite what the nations had previously agreed and what God had originally promised. 'Palestine' was the derogatory name given to the land by the Romans following the dispersal to rub Jewish noses in the dirt. It was in fact the name of their old enemies, the Philistines, whom David defeated with his sling!

When the Jews began resettling the area in the late 19th century, they came to a barren wasteland. And yet, in fulfilment of more ancient prophecies, it is now a fertile place that is filling the world with fruit, among other things. The relatively few Arabs who were living there at the time swelled in numbers as they saw opportunity for employment from the enterprising Jews, who were always happy to live side by side with their Arab neighbours, who came as labourers on the first agricultural kibbutzes. You only have to look at surveys taken among ordinary Palestinians to realise that they would rather live under Israeli rule than Arab. In fact there were always Jewish inhabitants in the land and if you go back to the 1800s there was virtually no Arab population there outside of Jerusalem, along the coast and around Galilee and the Jezreel Valley.

But surrounding nations attacked the new nation almost before it was born. Then they virtually invented a refugee crisis by encouraging local Arabs to flee their homes (and accusing the Jews of driving them out) while at the same time refusing to welcome them to their own countries.

This created a totally fake 'refugee' situation which made Israel look like the aggressors and raised sympathy for the need of a 'Palestinian' homeland. For at the same time as the world highlights the plight of Arab/Palestinian refugees there is no mention that at least as many, if not more, Jews have been evicted by Arab nations and assimilated by Israel with little or no fuss.

The real reason for all this subterfuge was that the Arab nations of the Middle East wanted to wipe Israel off the face of the earth, just as Hitler had intended. In fact Hitler had merely copied existing Arab measures against Jews, such as the use of the Yellow Star and the ban on Jews being allowed to own businesses. At any rate it's a spiritual battle, an ancient conflict of jealousy because God had seemed to favour one over the other – specifically, Isaac over Ishmael (Abraham's sons).

And the anti-Semitic trouble-makers have caused endless tension in the Middle East ever since. If it was all about so-called Israeli occupation, why is it that the Palestinians in Gaza, now free of Jews, have been launching rockets at civilians in Israel ever since the pull-out and have dug a 275-metre tunnel under the border to attack Israeli soldiers? Israel does want peace and needs security – if Hezbollah stopped fighting, there would be peace. But if Israel stopped fighting, there would be no Israel!

These tensions have also been prophesied – particularly by Ezekiel and Zechariah who wrote of terrifying events that would ultimately lead to the Battle of Armageddon. And just when all seems lost, the Messiah will return to judge the nations and usher in a 1,000-year reign of peace. Zechariah, writing many hundreds of years before Christ, said the Jewish people would "look on the one they have pierced" and mourn deeply for having rejected him.

However, as I said before, he has never rejected them and this would be a time when the whole nation would turn to their Messiah in fulfilment of God's ultimate plan for Jews and Gentiles to be reconciled into 'one new man' through the work of Christ on the cross. And all Israel would be reconciled to their God.

The restoration of the Jews is in two stages. A physical re-birth, which has already largely taken place with the re-settling of the land, especially since 1948, though not yet complete with Jews from Russia and elsewhere still finding their way back to the Holy Land, will be followed by a spiritual re-birth when they recognise the Messiah they have so far rejected and turn to him en masse.

Of course we are talking of rejection only in relative terms as it is often forgotten that the early church was almost entirely Jewish and that there were up to 100,000 Christians in Jerusalem alone within 25 years of the time of Christ. And now in these last days – we recognise the times in which we are living as such because they are a fulfilment of the signs Jesus himself gave to indicate his imminent return – a growing number of Jews have already recognised Jesus (Yeshua) as their Messiah, worshipping him along with Gentile Christians around the world. I have been to one such service myself where Sixties pop sensation Helen Shapiro was a member of the congregation. In fact there are more so-called 'Messianics' in Israel today that at any time since 70AD.

Tragically, however, there are sections of the church who have rejected the Jews, by which I mean they believe God has finished with them because of their sin and unbelief and replaced them with the Church. So all the promises originally applied to the Jews now find their fulfilment in the church, they say. But this line of thinking misunderstands the whole nature of God, for whom mercy triumphs over judgment. If God had rejected the Jews for their unbelief, what chance does the Church have with all her many sins and inconsistencies (not to say persecution of the Jews) over the centuries? Jesus prayed over his killers, "Father, forgive them, for they know not what they do." Do you think his prayer will go unanswered?

Israel may have stumbled over the issue of their Messiah, but they have not fallen. God has not rejected his people, but in the meantime has allowed Gentile believers to be 'grafted in' (see St Paul's Letter to the Romans chapter 11) to the Olive Tree that is Israel, so that our roots are in Judaism, through Jesus the Jew, who said "salvation is from the Jews". We don't support the root – the root supports us, St Paul explains. It is a closed heart and mind who believes that the Lord who inspired Paul to say that the gifts and calling of God are irrevocable (Romans 11) can then turn round and say, 'Yes, but I don't like you Jews anymore'. He would have to double-cross himself to do that, and I don't think that's likely.

The prophet Jeremiah wrote: "This is what the Lord says: 'Only if the heavens above can be measured and the foundations of the earth below be searched out will I reject all the descendants of Israel because of all they have done,' declares the Lord." (Jer 31.35-37) Let's also bear in mind that Jesus will return, not only to Jerusalem, but as the Lion of Judah, which surely requires him to be Jewish. Yes, he will still be a Jew! Salvation, prosperity and so much more has come to the world through the Jews – ultimately through Jesus Christ – and if you desire more than a second-hand blessing, you need to bow before the one who is not only King of the Jews, but King of Kings and Lord of Lords. And if we love Jesus, we will love the Jews.

Postscript

God is still in the business of leaving miraculous signs of his covenant with the Jews. At the height of the 2006 crisis in Lebanon, in which Israel retaliated to constant bombardment by terrorists with severe strikes on Hezbollah strongholds, news came of an ancient 20-page manuscript unearthed from an Irish bog, possibly dating back as far as 800AD. For a fragile document to have survived in such conditions for so long is surely a miracle. The book, in Latin script, was open at Psalm 83, which describes how Arab and Middle Eastern powers form a last-days' covenant against the God of Israel and against the Jewish people in order to wipe Israel off the face of the earth. "Come," they say, "let us destroy them as a nation, that the name of Israel be remembered no more (verse 4)." It's time to come to their aid, and align ourselves with the thinking of the God of Israel, the author of the Scriptures and the Father of our Lord Jesus Christ.

FOR FURTHER READING
'Britain: A Nation Called by God' published by Love Never Fails, PO Box 2687, Eastbourne BN22 7LZ. Also available from this address: 'For the Love of Zion' by Kelvin Crombie (£8) and 'The Forsaken Promise', a double DVD.

CHAPTER 2

Prophecies fulfilled

Just as the coming of the Messiah was prophesied through the Hebrew Scriptures (what Christians call the Old Testament), so the return to the Promised Land of Jewish people from every corner of the globe is also repeatedly foretold. That Jesus was the Messiah is still disputed by most of today's Jews, though obviously a significant body of them recognised him as such during his appearance on earth 2,000 years ago since the early church was built on the foundation of apostles and other leaders who were almost exclusively Jewish and, within a generation of Christ's death and resurrection, it is estimated that 100,000 people – half the population of Jerusalem at that time – were followers of Yeshua (as Jesus was called). And it was obviously vital for them that Jesus was clearly seen to have been the fulfilment of the ancient prophecies.

Many people are still familiar with the traditional nine lessons and carols held in the run-up to Christmas. The Old Testament lessons include Isaiah's prophecies – some 600 years before Christ – that He would be born of a virgin (chapter 7, verse 14) and that his ministry would be centred in Galilee (ch 9, v 2-6) while Micah added that he would be born in Bethlehem as a descendant of King David (ch 5, v2).

Isaiah also predicted very specific aspects surrounding his death (chapters 52-53) also echoed in the Psalms (22) such as "he was pierced for our transgressions..." and "he did not open his mouth; he was led like a lamb to the slaughter..." and what about, "he was assigned a grave with the wicked (Jesus was crucified between two thieves) and with the rich in his death" (he was buried in the tomb of Joseph of Arimathea, a wealthy relative who also became a committed follower of Jesus. ...And how about this? "After the suffering of his soul, he will see the light of life and be satisfied."

From Psalm 22, we read: "I am poured out like water, and all my bones are out of joint" (v14), "... they have pierced my hands and my feet" (v16) and "they divide my garments among them and cast lots for my clothing". The Apostle John records in his gospel that "when (the soldiers) came to Jesus and found that he was already dead, they did not break his legs", fulfilling the scripture that not one of his bones would be broken (see Exodus 12.46, Numbers 9.12 & Psalm 34.20). "Instead, one of the soldiers pierced Jesus' side with a spear, bringing a sudden flow of blood and water." Crucifixion would of course have involved nails being driven through his hands and feet and Matthew records in his gospel that "when they had crucified him, they divided up his clothes by casting lots."

These are just a few selections, but it has been worked out that the mathematical chances of just eight of 25 such prophecies being fulfilled in one man are one in ten to the 17th power – or 1 in 100,000,000,000,000,000 (see *Abandoned* by Stan Telchin, page 148, published by Marshall Pickering). In other words, the prophets were clearly inspired by divine wisdom. And the writers of the New Testament go to great lengths to demonstrate how Christ was a fulfilment of the ancient Jewish prophecies because it was seen as essential to building a strong foundation for their faith. Matthew, in particular, seemed to have Jewish readers in mind when writing his gospel. And so he starts in a very Jewish way with a record of Christ's genealogy. He mentions the scriptures we have outlined above along with many others to back up the disciples' claims for having found the One for whom the nation had been waiting for so long.

One of the first disciples was Nathanael, who confessed his belief shortly after being told by Philip: "We have found the one Moses wrote about in the Law, and about whom the prophets also wrote – Jesus of Nazareth, the son of Joseph." But he was initially sceptical, asking: "Nazareth! Can anything good come from there?" So Philip encouraged him to "come and see", and when Jesus saw him approaching, he said of him: "Here is a true Israelite, in whom there is nothing false." And when he realised Jesus knew everything about him, he became the first follower (even ahead of Peter) to confess the truth about Christ. "Rabbi, you are the Son of God; you are the King of Israel."

And then there was the account of the two disciples on the road to Emmaus recorded by Luke (the only gospel writer who may not have been a Jew). The risen Jesus (at first unrecognised by them) drew alongside them and joined in their conversation in which they were expressing their devastation over the crucifixion of the one they believed had come to redeem Israel. Then Jesus said: "How foolish you are, and how slow of heart to believe all that the prophets have spoken! Did not the Messiah have to suffer these things and then enter his glory? And beginning with Moses and all the Prophets, he explained to them what was said in all the Scriptures concerning himself." (Luke 24.25-27)

They invited Jesus to stay, and finally recognised him when he broke the bread as he had done at the 'Last Supper' – an event clearly not restricted to the twelve, as famous paintings and the like might have led us to believe. There were undoubtedly many more disciples present, including some of the women who had supported Jesus throughout his ministry. That Passover meal of all Passover meals saw Jesus break bread and pour wine as symbols of what he was about to achieve by dying for our sins on the cross and thus inaugurating the New Covenant of direct access to God through a personal relationship with his Son for all who would identify with him in recognising the eternal life won through his broken body and shed blood.

But although Jesus came for the whole world, the message he brought was "for the Jew first", indicated by his comment recorded in John's gospel that salvation was from the Jews and emphasised three times by St Paul in his letter to the Romans. And of course he was not in fact rejected by the Jews as a whole, but by the chief priests, though obviously this did create a sense of national rejection, as Jesus himself recognised, since they represented the religious leadership of a theocratic nation chosen by God.

Scattered among the nations

Nevertheless, God still had a plan for his people and his promises to them would be fulfilled because he always kept his word (see Romans 11.29). They may have become prodigals, but he would welcome them back as a loving Father. And so we come to examine some of the many promises relating to how the Jewish people, dispersed throughout the nations (not just to Babylon as happened shortly afterwards) would return to their ancient homeland in the latter days. As with the confession of Nathanael, "You are the Son of God; the King of Israel", the coming of Jesus has a significance for both heaven (Son of God) and earth (King of Israel), though that is not to say Israel's future should be seen only in the natural, physical, earthly sense rather than having a spiritual dimension, for it was always God's purpose that the nation should return to his ways and be a "light to the Gentiles".

When the prophets foretold the dispersion of the Jews to every corner of the globe, it could only have been divinely inspired as they could never have imagined how that would come about in the natural – though of course they knew that God would not tolerate their continuing disobedience. And yet their emphasis was not on God's judgment as much as on his compassion in bringing them back and restoring them to a full appreciation of his love for them. They warned that there would come a time when, because of their diso-bedience to God's law, he would allow enemies to overwhelm them and carry them away to exile, a scenario that occurred in 586 BC when the Babylonians invaded their land and took them into captivity. Many will recall the modern pop song by the group Bony M, 'By the Rivers of Babylon… how could we sing the songs of Zion in a foreign land?' Actually, it's an ancient song taken straight from the Hebrew Scriptures recounting their time of misery away from the Promised Land. But in the fullness of time (after 70 years) the Jews were allowed to return to their beloved homeland and rebuild the walls of Jerusalem under the prophet Nehemiah.

However, this initial banishment was nothing compared to what was to come following the destruction of the Temple in Jerusalem by the Romans in AD 70 – just a generation after Jesus walked among them and in fulfilment of his own prophecy relating to the temple that "not one stone would be left upon another". This sparked the scattering of the Jewish people throughout the world. Of course the prophets will have had no idea how this would come about, but wrote with obvious divine insight about events some 2,500 years into the future when they foretold how God, in his love and compassion, would one day bring them back to their ancient homeland from all four corners of the earth.

For those who suggest that the Church has replaced Israel in God's affections because of their initial rejection of the Messiah, the following excerpts categorically disprove that notion because it is clear that the return from Babylon (just one country) is not particularly in mind as time and again we read that they will return from the north, south, east and west, and "from every nation to which the Lord has banished them." Here are just a few of them:

"He will raise a banner for the nations and gather the exiles of Israel; he will assemble the scattered people of Judah from the four quarters of the earth." (Isaiah 11.12)

"In days to come Jacob will take root, Israel will bud and blossom and fill all the world with fruit." (Isaiah 27.6)

"Do not be afraid, for I am with you; I will bring your children from the east and gather you from the west. I will say to the north, 'Give them up!' and to the south, 'Do not hold them back.' (Isaiah 43.5f)

"The days are coming when men will no longer say, 'As surely as the Lord lives, who brought the Israelites up out of Egypt,' but they will say, 'As surely as the Lord lives, who brought the Israelites up out of the land of the north and out of all the countries where he had banished them.' For I will restore them to the land I gave to their forefathers." (Jeremiah 16.14f)

Ezekiel records: "This is what the Sovereign Lord says: I will gather you from the nations and bring you back from the countries where you have been scattered, and I will give you back the land of Israel again." (Ezek 11.17)

And Amos records the Lord as saying: "I will bring back my exiled people Israel; they will rebuild the ruined cities and live in them. They will plant vineyards and drink their wine; they will make gardens and eat their fruit. I will plant Israel in their own land, never again to be uprooted from the land I have given them." (Amos 9.14f)

Those who were well acquainted with the Scriptures – including leading British politicians like William Wilberforce, Lord Balfour and others, made it their business to facilitate the return to their ancient homeland of the Jewish people (since it was so clearly in God's purpose) – but tragically it took the attempted annihilation of the Jewish race by the Nazis in the 1930s and 40s to provoke sufficient sympathy for their cause which was to pave the way for the re-birth of Israel in 1948. It was hardly a viable state at first in view of the relatively small number of Jews living in the land, but the ancient prophecies soon began to be fulfilled as Jews from every nation under heaven returned to Israel so that now there are at least as many Jews within the land (over seven million) as there are still scattered throughout the world.

And this process of 'Aliyah' (returning home) continues unabated as planeloads and shiploads arrive on a regular basis. This has included more than a million Russian Jews, for whom even a serious language barrier has not dissuaded them from returning to their roots. And Christians have been at the forefront of helping sometimes poor and oppressed Jewish people in foreign lands obtain the necessary documents, transport and finance to make this amazing journey.

And the language barrier has sparked another miracle of modern Israel – the re-birth after 2,000 years of ancient Hebrew which has proved a great uniting force among Israelis. Though a nation dispersed and assimilated among many, they are now being re-gathered into a united people once again.

Gathered from the nations

Aliyah began in earnest soon after the re-birth of Israel in 1948 when Operation Magic Carpet brought 47,000 Jews out of Yemen between June 1949 and September 1950. In a secret airlift also known as Wings of Eagles and Messiah's Coming, British and American transport planes made some 380 flights from Aden in response to an increasingly perilous situation for the Yemenite Jewish community there.

Following the 1947 UN Partition Plan granting a homeland for the Jews as well as a separate state for Arabs in the area (Trans-Jordan), 82 people were killed and a number of Jewish homes destroyed as a result of Muslim riots in Aden. Then, early in 1948, accusations of the murder of two Muslim Yemeni girls led to the looting of Jewish property and Aden's Jewish community became economically paralysed as most of their stores and businesses were destroyed. And so, in response to an increasingly dangerous situation, the overwhelming majority of Yemenite Jews were secretly airlifted to Israel. Most had never seen an aircraft before – hence the operation's nickname – with many refusing to board out of fear before being reassured when their rabbi reminded them of the biblical origin of its official name – "You yourselves have seen what I did to Egypt, and how I bore you on wings of eagles, and brought you to myself." (Exodus 19.4) And from Isaiah 40.31: "But those who hope in the Lord will renew their strength. They will soar on wings like eagles; they will run and not grow weary, they will walk and not be faint." It was the first in a series of operations whose purpose was to transport entire communities of Jews from Arab countries to Israel en masse during the 1950s and 1960s.

Also in 1950, Operation Ezra and Nehemiah saw a massive 120,000 Jews emigrate to Israel from Iraq, where the Jews were taken during the Babylonian captivity in the sixth century before Christ, while 75,000 came from North Africa from 1948-54. Then in 1984, Operation Moses saw 14,500 Jews airlifted from Ethiopia in just 36 hours, the name reflecting its similarity with the exodus from Egypt led by Moses. And because Jews were forbidden to leave the country, it was again necessary for the operation to remain clandestine.

During the 1990s one million Jews made Aliyah to Israel from the former Soviet Union, many with the help of Christian organisations working with the Jewish Agency, and they also came from Syria, Albania, North and South America, Great Britain, Australia, New Zealand, and a good number (some 80,000) from France, where anti-Semitism is becoming increasingly evident again, especially from the large Muslim community. A total of over three million Jews have returned to the Promised Land since 1948, contributing to nearly half Israel's 7.2 million citizens.

Just one of the Christian groups, Operation Exodus (a ministry of the Ebenezer Emergency Fund), has helped 130,000 Jews return to Israel over the past 20 years.

Return of the Jews – a modern miracle

And with calls for a boycott of Israeli goods coinciding with a rise in anti-Semitism, it is not surprising that a planeload of Jews have recently left Britain for the Holy Land. This was the first mass aliyah from the UK, a significant development in which all ages were represented with young people going despite knowing they would have to serve in the army.

Meanwhile Israeli MPs called for a boycott of British goods amid claims that new government advice on labelling supermarket produce from the West Bank recalled the Nazi persecution of the Jews. And it immediately attracted the support of nearly half the Knesset, Israel's parliament. The British Government advice suggested how supermarkets could use labels distinguishing between Palestinian produce and that grown by Israeli settlers in the 'occupied' West Bank. At the same time a London court briefly sanctioned the arrest of former Israeli Foreign Minister Tzipi Livni for alleged war crimes – but she decided against visiting Britain.

The return of Jews to the land of Israel is one of the true wonders of the modern world. Many more are still eager to come but, because of anti-Semitism, lots of Jewish people in Russia changed their names and destroyed their papers. Proof of identity is needed before they can be accepted into Israel as *olim* (returnees) and Christian organisations like Ebenezer assist with obtaining finance and the necessary documents. There are also still 8,000 Falasha Jews in Ethiopia waiting in poverty to be allowed back to Israel. And a city is being built in the Negev area to make room for the return of Jews from South America where anti-Semitism is also rising.

Even the USA, which has the largest proportion of Jews outside Israel, has recently witnessed a big increase in aliyah which could be connected with growing financial insecurity along with a tempering of support for Israel under a President who is perceived as pro-Muslim.

As already pointed out, the aliyah was widely predicted by the Old Testament prophets – long before the Jews had been dispersed throughout the world following the destruction of Jerusalem by the Romans in AD 70 – who said that the phenomenon would be regarded as an even greater miracle than the crossing of the Red Sea on dry land as they escaped from slavery in Egypt. And the Bible makes clear that their physical return – as yet incomplete – will be followed by their spiritual revival and recognition of the Messiah the nation as a whole rejected at his first coming. For Ezekiel also writes: "I will give you a new heart and put a new spirit in you; I will remove from you your heart of stone and give you a heart of flesh." This great national event would usher in the Second Coming of Christ. Looking ahead to that time, Zechariah foretells: "They will look on me, the one they have pierced, and they will mourn for him as one mourns for an only child…"

Jesus, the Jew, will return as a Jew – and woe-betide those nations who have been party to persecution of his people, or who have engaged in political compromise at their expense. And if we as individuals wish to be ready to welcome him back, we need also to ensure we have a right heart and attitude towards his people.

If you love Jesus, you will love the Jews.

CHAPTER 3

Feasts fulfilled

At the risk of courting controversy, I have to say the attitude of some Christians to alcohol – and certainly that generally perceived by the watching public – is seriously at odds with that prevailing at the time the Old and New Testaments were written. And Jesus' first recorded miracle – at the wedding in Cana of Galilee – is the clearest example of how wine in particular played an important and indeed noble part in Jewish culture. Jesus not only blessed the couple with his gracious presence but, when the wine ran out – a great embarrassment for the hosts – he made sure the party continued by turning several huge jars of water into wine; and the very best wine at that, as the master of ceremonies pointed out in wonder. It's a real shame that many Christians seem to have been turning wine into water ever since.

But our Lord wasn't just validating the drinking of alcohol or performing a party trick. He was declaring in no uncertain terms who he was. For on every Jewish Sabbath (Shabbat), which starts on Friday evening each week, the blessing of the wine at dinner is followed by the prayer of thanksgiving said by all present at the table: "Blessed are you, O Lord our God, King of the Universe, who created the fruit of the vine. Amen!" Translated, our Jewish friends say: *"Baruch atah Adonai Eloheinu, Melech Ha olam, boray pri hagafen. Amen!"*

By turning water into wine, Jesus demonstrated in the profoundest way possible that he was indeed God! Wow! Can you imagine the impact that must have made on those wedding guests who understood what he was in fact saying? As Aaron Eime, a Messianic Jewish leader in Jerusalem, points out: "He has just said, 'I am the King of the Universe'." Aaron also makes the point that, by joining the wedding festivities, Jesus demonstrated God's involvement in human affairs – both in their fun times and in their tragedies, as when he wept over the death of his friend Lazarus – unlike the Essenes, a Jewish sect that existed around the time of Christ who retreated to the desert in order to

29

escape from the world.

As for the Sabbath itself, it was designed as a time of rest from work when thoughts could be turned to family, faith and the fellowship involved in sharing food at the table in celebration of all God's goodness. It was given as one of the Ten Commandments but, though the Jewish people have largely kept this important ritual which has in turn helped to keep them together as a people, the Gentile world has effectively thrown out the principle with 24/7 shopping, working all hours and no time to stop and think about family, God or even our own health (which is severely affected when regular rest is not taken), not to mention what life is all about.

Anyone who has experienced long hours of work over a protracted period will know what I mean. The body begins to break down – physically, mentally, emotionally and spiritually – when placed under such stress. But the command to rest was not given as an unbending principle to prevent you from attending to essentials or emergencies as Jesus pointed out to his critics after he healed sick people on the Sabbath. "The Sabbath was made for man, not man for the Sabbath," he scolded them. It's for our own good; for our health and well-being both spiritually and physically. And as the Scriptures declare, Jesus is our 'Sabbath rest' (Hebrews 4) – he is the epitome of the perfect rest and peace we can ever know. He was the One who said: "Come to me, all who are weary and burdened, and I will give you rest." (Matthew 11.28)

Jesus was the "hope of Israel", as the Apostle Paul explained to the Jewish leaders in Rome where he was under house arrest. We are told: "From morning till evening he explained and declared to them the kingdom of God and tried to convince them about Jesus from the Law of Moses and from the Prophets." (Acts 28.23b) He was not making it up; this was no new religion, but a fulfilment of the old with which they were familiar.

Earlier in Acts (Luke's account of the fledgling church), we are told of the occasion when Philip was led by the Spirit to speak to an important Ethiopian official returning from a pilgrimage to Jerusalem who was reading a famous passage from the book of the prophet Isaiah which starts, "He was led like a sheep to the slaughter, as a lamb before his shearer is silent…" (Isaiah 53.7) The official wanted to know to whom the prophet was referring. And Philip "began with that very passage of Scripture and told him the good news about Jesus." (Acts 8.35)

It was also Luke in his gospel who recorded the account of the two despondent disciples on the road to Emmaus who at first did not recognise the risen Lord when he drew alongside them and joined in their conversation. After listening them out as they vented their crushing disappointment that the one they had hoped would save Israel from the occupying Romans had been crucified, Jesus said to them: "How foolish you are, and how slow of heart to believe all that the prophets have spoken! Did not the Christ (Messiah) have to suffer these things and then enter his glory?" And beginning with Moses and all the Prophets, he explained to them what was said in all the Scriptures concerning himself. (Luke 24.25-7) And it's worth pointing out that the fact Jesus was the ultimate fulfilment of the Jewish Scriptures was so clearly emphasised by possibly the only non-Jewish author of the Bible's 66 books!

Encounter with Jesus

Not long ago my wife Linda had a vivid and very powerful dream, and I soon knew all about it as she woke me up in the early hours of the morning.

"Charles, I've been with Jesus!" she gasped in a loud whisper (we were on our mobile blow-up bed in the lounge of her sister's family home where we were staying at the time and she obviously didn't want to wake up the children).

There was quite a bit more to her dream than I will share here, but a key aspect of it is particularly apt to our discussion of the feasts.

She went on: "Although there were others there whom I knew, I was talking face to face with Jesus. He spoke about some members of the family, and how he had been there for them at special times of crisis in their lives without them even realising it.

"Anyway, he was very relaxed and I noticed he was drinking from a large tankard. I suppose I was expecting him to be drinking wine, or perhaps tea. And he must have realised what I was thinking and chuckled to himself before it became clear that he was actually drinking beer! And it must have been a two-pint pot!

"After telling me he didn't think much of the tea there anyway, he asked me a question, as of course Jewish teachers are in the habit of doing: 'What does it say in the Scriptures?'

"And then I remembered what he said at the Last Supper: 'I will not drink of this fruit of the vine from now on until that day when I drink it anew with you in my Father's kingdom.' (Matthew 26.29)

"It was an amazing revelation."

And we were so taken up with what had clearly been a divine encounter that it was some time before we drifted back to sleep.

Jesus is joy personified, and he certainly enjoys a party, but for the moment, it seems, he's having to make do with real ale (which tastes very good anyway if you haven't tried it). Yet he's longing to share the cup of wine with us at his coming again when he finally welcomes the Bride of Christ (the Church) into his loving arms at what the Bible calls the Marriage Feast of the Lamb.

Vision in Cana

Linda also had an amazing experience at Cana of Galilee during her second trip to Israel in the year 2000. And it is because it was so vivid and real that we got married. Jesus' attendance at the wedding in Cana has inspired lovers down the centuries and is read as part of the Church of England marriage service. As Linda was representing her church on a tour involving Christians from the Sheffield diocese, she had been asked to pray for various members at appropriate points and so obviously marriage was an issue when she visited the church at Cana, where she duly lifted up the needs of couples who were going through difficulties. While there she was watching some monks playing the guitar and singing praise songs to God when suddenly she had a vision of her own wedding, and she could see her groom, though his back was turned. This was a startling experience for a 43-year-old who had never been married, although she had been half-prepared for it by an earlier prophecy from a performing artist, who was being hosted by her church and who told her that God was going to bring someone special into her life.

Within five months of her Cana vision, Linda had met the man she was to marry. And for me, too, it was a prophecy fulfilled as, within days of the funeral of my late wife Irene, a friend called Dennis Penhearow phoned me to apologise for not having made the service on account of his ill health. He was an elderly man who saw his main ministry as one of intercession for the needs of others and, while he was praying for me, he saw a vision of Irene looking down from heaven and smiling, 'letting me go' as it were. The message he conveyed to me was that I would be married again soon, and that I would know who it was before the end of the year. I met Linda on a blind date on November 18 2000 and had proposed to her – and been accepted – well before Christmas!

Jewish ancestry

I am part-Jewish myself and always believed – as most evangelical Christians seemed to have done until more recent times – that the New Testament was a fulfilment of the Old, that Jesus was the Jewish Messiah despite apparently not being recognised by the majority of his people at the time, and that the Old Testament prophecies relating to the Jews would one day be literally fulfilled. And all this was confirmed through the influence of Helen McIntosh, a wonderful Jewish lady who led the 'Nursery Class' for seekers and new believers at All Souls Church, Langham Place, London, in the 1970s. The class was devised by our rector, Rev John Stott, and was a kind of forerunner of the hugely influential Alpha Course later started at Holy Trinity, Brompton, a few miles away. Helen soon took me under her wing as her assistant and was effectively my spiritual 'mother'. And she always referred to herself as a 'completed Jew' rather than a Christian because she had found the Messiah who had been promised so long ago to the Jewish people and who would at the same time be a 'light to the Gentiles'.

For my part, my mother's maternal ancestors belonged to the Sephardic Jewish community in Portugal (otherwise known as Latin Jews found in North Africa and the Spanish peninsula) before being driven out by persecution like so many other Jewish communities in Europe over the centuries. But they found a welcome in America, initially settling in New Orleans before my great-grandfather joined his brother in Jamaica where he set up a thriving tobacco business. But it all went up in smoke – not just the business premises, but the whole of Kingston, the capital – in the great earthquake of 1904. He had married an Irish Catholic, and they had nine children, one of whom was my Gran Minola with whom I lived in London for several years and who regaled me with many tales of that very frightening event she experienced as a nine-year-old, alone in the house at the time the 'quake struck. But she also had many happy memories of idyllic, lazy days on the beaches of that beautiful Caribbean island with its lush vegetation and tropical climate cooled by the Gulf Stream breezes.

A matriarchal figure who could charm the hardest of cases, yet whom we all found so hard to please, gran did not follow Jewish customs, or Catholic ones for that matter, often confessing to me that she prayed every night 'just in case'. In fact she verbally persecuted me for my faith but grew more open to the possibility of the Lord being there for her as she grew older. And my mum tells me that, as she lay sick and dying in her last days, she would frequently cry out 'Lord, have mercy!' I trust that he was indeed there for her, and I thank God for my Jewish heritage. For one thing, it was thanks to gran's sharp business brain that we benefited from so many material blessings as a family. We've had a family home in the heart of much sought-after Hampstead for over 77 years and she even helped my doctor dad with the purchase of a downtown surgery in the South African town where I grew up. All of which neatly leads us back to our discussion of the feasts.

CHAPTER 4

The ultimate Passover sacrifice

As Jews around the world celebrate Passover each year, a growing number of them are also now marking the occasion by worshipping Jesus, whom they believe is the ultimate fulfilment of this feast. Sixties pop sensation Helen Shapiro, for one, believes the Passover was totally fulfilled with the coming of Jesus Christ.

For a Jewess, that is a very politically incorrect, not to say religiously rocky, statement. But her own personal discovery of the reality of the risen Christ has turned her into a bold witness for the Christian gospel which has its roots deeply embedded in Judaism.

It was a few years ago that she began the Jewish Passover celebration by telling a Yorkshire audience that she had found the Messiah. Addressing a packed school hall near Selby in North Yorkshire, the London-born singer told of her life-changing experience when she came "face to face with Jesus" whom she once thought of as the God of the Christians. And during a long evening in which she juggled the roles of evangelist, pastor, worship leader and teacher, she explained how the Feast of Passover was ultimately fulfilled by Jesus' death on the cross. It was originally inaugurated to remind the Israelites how God had miraculously delivered them from bondage in Egypt.

Pharaoh had repeatedly refused to let them go despite a series of plagues sent to punish his stubbornness but, when the tenth plague struck – killing the first-born of all who had not placed the blood of a sacrificial lamb on the doorpost of their houses – they were finally set free from their slavery. God had promised through Moses: "When I see the blood, the angel of death will pass over you." Jesus was the ultimate 'Lamb of God', sacrificed for the sins of the world – and all who put their trust in his redeeming blood would be set free from bondage to sin and self and inherit eternal life.

Brought up in London's East End, Helen became a star as a young teenager in the early sixties with a string of hit singles including *Walking Back to Happiness*. And in early 1963 the Beatles joined her tour as a supporting act! Then, some 25 years ago, she read a book called *Betrayed* by Stan Telchin, in which the Jewish author told how he was horrified when his daughter came home one day to say she had come to believe Jesus was their Messiah. He set out to prove she was wrong and became a believer himself instead.

Helen too was powerfully captivated by the book through which she came to see that the Hebrew Bible was liberally dosed with messianic prophecies (over 300) clearly fulfilled in Christ. And that the New Testament was not written by an Englishman, even though the names – such as James, John and Jesus – had been anglicised. "I came face to face with Jesus," she said. "I was drawn to him like a magnet. I couldn't take my eyes off him. He was still blessing people when raised on the cross."

But it was not an easy transformation, especially with childhood memories of being taunted in the school playground with accusations of "You killed Jesus". Now in her sixties, Helen wowed the audience with many Jewish-style songs in praise of Messiah – there were song-sheets allowing the audience to join in – drawing attention away from herself to the One she clearly loved above all else. She also sang *Walking Back to Happiness*, and told her story in between.

"There were no lightning flashes; just a knowing that it was real," she said about the moment she committed her life to Christ at 10.30pm on August 26 1987. "I guess that was my dead spirit coming alive. I knew without a shadow of a doubt that Jesus was the fulfilment of every messianic prophecy in the Hebrew Bible, and was therefore the Messiah."

But it did not mean she was no longer a Jew – he was in fact a fulfilment of her Jewish-ness. "Jesus was Jewish, and still is. When a Jewish person receives Jesus they are returning to the God of Abraham."

Helen recorded her first hit in 1961 at the age of 14 with *Don't Treat Me Like a Child*. It was heady stuff for a kid and God went on the back-burner – she had grown up in a loving Jewish community with an obvious belief in God. But it was with the onset of the hippie movement in the late sixties that she renewed an interest in spiritual things by dabbling in the occult – indulging in psychic phenomena involving mediums, fortune-telling and the like.

She was first drawn to Christ through her musical director, a top-flight professional musician who was prepared to give it all up to become a preacher. "I envied his faith and I wanted what he had, so I started thinking about this Jesus. Lying on my bed, I asked, 'Jesus, are you really the Messiah? If you are, please show me.' I wasn't sure if I wouldn't be struck by lightning, but everywhere I went in the ensuing weeks I bumped into things connected with Jesus."

And it was then, after flying home from a concert in Germany, that Bob (her musical director) gave her the book *Betrayed*, which quotes numerous messianic prophecies about the coming of the Messiah and through which she was amazed to discover, for example, that Psalm 22 was a picture of Jesus on the cross written a thousand years earlier by King David at a time when there was no such thing as crucifixion. She confirmed all these discoveries by reading the Hebrew Bible.

Then she read the New Testament – "the bit on the end that shouldn't be there, forbidden to Jews. So imagine my surprise when I turned to Matthew's gospel and found the most Jewish thing I'd seen outside of the Old Testament – the genealogy of Jesus." And she read on to discover how Christ fulfilled one messianic prophecy after another. She was totally convinced and became a believer. And having dabbled in the occult, she knew once she'd found Jesus that she had to get rid of all her paraphernalia on the subject.

Helen is living testimony to the biblical truth predicting a growing latter-day recognition of Messiah among Jews. She ended the evening with the challenge that there was a heaven to be gained and a hell to be shunned, that Jesus (*Yeshua* in Hebrew) was the only way to God and that he was coming back to judge the world. Are you ready?

Other key feasts

Shavuot (also known as the Feast of Weeks or Pentecost) falls 50 days after Passover, celebrates the first fruits of the harvest (wheat, barley, grapes, figs, pomegranates, olives and dates) and is fulfilled on the Day of Pentecost (50 days after Christ's crucifixion) with the birth of the Church following the response of 3,000 people to the outpouring of the Holy Spirit and the message of Peter that Jesus was the long-promised Messiah who had come to fulfil all their hopes and dreams. It was thus the first 'harvest' of souls for the kingdom of God under the New Covenant through which, through the cross, sins could be forgiven and a relationship with God established on a personal and permanent basis.

But Shavuot is also traditionally (as encouraged by the Rabbis) the anniversary of the giving of the Law (Ten Commandments) to Moses on Mt Sinai and, on this level, is also perfectly fulfilled in Yeshua who came, not to abolish the Law and the Prophets, but to fulfil them, as he stated so clearly in the Sermon on the Mount (Matthew 5.17). In fact he had come to "write the Law on our hearts" (Ezekiel 36.26). So Jesus had come to fulfil the law and write it on our hearts, not just on tablets of stone, to enable us the more easily to follow its precepts, and he spelt it out on the 'mount', as his Father had done for Moses.

Sukkot, or the Feast of Tabernacles, is a celebration once again of the

Exodus from Egypt in the 13th century BC with specific emphasis on the 40 years in the Wilderness when they lived 'under the stars' and God protected and provided for them in miraculous ways such as the sending down of 'heavenly manna' for daily food and water from the rock. And so today Jews still mark this time by building temporary shelters out of palm branches and the like to remind them of God's provision and, indeed, their dependence on him – and, I suppose, the temporary nature of our lives on this planet in the light of the eternal significance of our souls and of God's kingdom.

It is also associated with the harvest (the full harvest resulting from the latter rains as opposed to the early spring rains) – a festival still widely marked in Christian communities. But there is also a deeper, spiritual significance as the Bible speaks of a latter-day 'harvest of the earth' when the sheep will be separated from the goats, when all men will have to give an account of what they've done and Jesus, the Judge of all mankind, will oversee the reaping of the good and bad crop as angels swing their sickles throughout the earth (Revelation 14.14-20). It is for this reason that the Second Coming of Christ is widely expected to take place during the Feast of Tabernacles. In any case, we know for sure that his coming is near when there is much trouble, anxiety, violence and injustice in the world. We would do well to act on our Lord's warning: "Be always on the watch, and pray that you may be able to escape all that is about to happen, and that you may be able to stand before the Son of Man." (Luke 21.36)

A light in the darkness

Hannukah is an eight-day Jewish festival celebrated close to Christmas (appropriately though not intentionally) to mark God's miraculous intervention at the time of the reign of the ruthless Syrian-Greek emperor Antiochus Epiphanes who desecrated the Jewish Temple by sacrificing a pig there and blasphemously proclaimed himself God. Judah Maccabee led a brave and successful revolt against the tyrant in 139 BC and re-established temple worship (Hannukah means 'dedication') with the aid of the menorah (seven-branched candlestick) which burned miraculously for eight days despite having only enough oil for a day. The Greeks had polluted the rest. In my opinion the feast also foreshadows the coming of the Jewish Messiah Yeshua (Jesus), described as "the light of the world", and I'm sure it's no coincidence that it falls around the same time as Christmas when much of the world is lit up with elaborate decorations to commemorate his birth some 2,000 years ago. Messianic Jews (who *do* believe Jesus is their Messiah) celebrate both feasts and it is interesting to note that the sight of a menorah as part of the festive decorations is becoming increasingly common.

And so at a time when billions of people celebrate the coming of light into the world in the person of Jesus Christ, a dark evil is threatening to engulf the very place of his birth and there is a need to sound the alarm. But as we were reminded in a Christmas card from the staff at the Jews for Jesus organisation, the baby born at Bethlehem is the only hope for peace in the Middle East.

Today we have an even greater threat to Israel in the form of Iran who, in defiance of America and most of the civilized world, has brazenly announced not only that it will continue its nuclear programme, but that it also plans to expand it with the building of an additional ten uranium enrichment plants. And all the while its president keeps threatening to destroy Israel! His country's nuclear ambitions are not only a direct threat to Israel, but also to the whole of the Middle East and to world peace itself.

As Michael Evans of the Jerusalem Prayer Team* says: "Rather than placing this enriched uranium in traditional nuclear missiles, which can easily be traced back to their source, Iran is likely to distribute this material through the terrorist networks it sponsors – Hamas and Hezbollah – and urge them to use it as so-called 'dirty bombs' against civilian populations in Israel and America. To the radical Islamic extremists running Iran, the death of hundreds of thousands of innocents is a small price to pay for uniting the world under Sharia Law (a strict, indeed ruthless, Muslim code) and Islamic rule. There is no question that they will use their nuclear programme for military purposes. I have been briefed by top Israeli and American intelligence and military experts on this subject, and I can tell you today that they are very worried by this threat."

There is speculation that Israeli Prime Minister Benjamin Netanyahu received some level of American approval for military action against Iran if they continue to defy international demands to halt their nuclear programme. But the price of any such co-operation could well be an imposed peace deal with the Palestinians.

Meanwhile there is the ever-present threat of war from Hezbollah on Israel's northern border. Consistent reports of an imminent war have been received by informed sources who say that a new cabinet in Lebanon has declared Hezbollah an authorised armed force to battle against Israel. "That means that if we go to war against Hezbollah we are going to war against Lebanon," the sources added.

A German-owned cargo ship carrying a huge Iranian arms shipment (apparently destined for Hezbollah forces in south Lebanon) was intercepted off the Cyprus coast by Israeli naval vessels acting on information provided by the United States. The massive weapons cache, including rockets capable of hitting most of Israel, was later displayed at the port of Ashdod for inspection by foreign diplomats.

And so the spectre of Armageddon looms each year at the same time the world focuses on the coming of the 'Prince of Peace', so named by the Jewish prophet Isaiah when he foretold how people walking in darkness would see "a great light". And he went on to announce triumphantly: "For unto us a child is born, unto us a Son is given, and the government shall be upon his shoulders, and his name will be called Wonderful Counsellor, Mighty God, Everlasting Father, Prince of Peace."

Armageddon is a reality; there will come a time, possibly not far away, when the nations of the earth will clash in a catastrophic battle on the plains of Megiddo in Israel – the Bible makes this clear. But then the Messiah will return in power and great glory to put an end to war and usher in a thousand-year reign of absolute peace.

Alison Barnett of Jews for Jesus, explaining the feast of Hannukah, said: "That is why each year we kindle our lamps, one light for each of the eight nights," adding: "The Hannukah Menorah has nine branches and we light eight of the branches with the ninth candle, the *shammas* or servant candle. The light of the menorah reminds us of our Messiah Jesus, who claimed to be the light of the world and, in the *shammas* candle, we see a picture of Jesus, of whom the Apostle John said: 'The true light that gives light to every man was coming into the world.'

"We can't help but see the connection between the light of Hannukah and the light that pierced the darkness when Yeshua (Jesus) was born. During this Hannukah and Christmas season, let us remember that the light of the world, the Servant King, has come into the world to bring hope and life to all who believe."

Sadly, some Orthodox Jews, like the Pharisees of old failing to recognise Jesus as their Messiah, are acting against those of their race who do believe – known worldwide as Messianic believers. A young boy called Ami Ortiz was terribly injured by a bomb which arrived at his home in the form of a 'gift' to celebrate the feast of Purim, marking the Jews' deliverance from annihilation by the Persian (Iranian) king through Queen Esther.

As Jesus was misunderstood, so are his followers. But he *is* the light of the world, and *will* bring peace on earth. That does not, however, justify indifference and lack of action on the part of our politicians who need unequivocally to demonstrate their support for Israel in defending itself against state-sponsored terrorism at this dangerous time.

FOOTNOTES

*A movement supporting Israel with prayer, information and action – especially in helping the poor.

CHAPTER 5

Britain's key role in Israel's story

As politicians agonise over the seemingly intractable problems of the Middle East, believers are watching a remarkable peace process taking place before their eyes. And at the heart of the solution, which has so far apparently escaped the notice of world leaders, is a growing movement of so-called Messianic Jews who believe Yeshua (Jesus) is their long-promised Messiah.

But key to the emergence of this group, along with the restoration of Jews to the Holy Land as a whole, is a 200-year-old missionary organisation – the Church's Ministry among Jewish people. Established in 1809 partly through the influence of men like William Wilberforce, CMJ became largely responsible for the re-establishment of a homeland for the Jews, influencing the Government of the time to work towards this goal.

And, as history records, it finally came about through the Balfour Declaration of 1917 followed by the granting of the British mandate over Palestine by the League of Nations in 1922 and then, in 1948, the recognition by the United Nations of the new state of Israel.

Robin Aldridge, former chief executive officer of CMJ UK, explained that it all began in the late 18th century with an influx of Jewish immigrants into the East End of London. They were mainly from France where they had come under persecution along with the protestant Huguenots. The new arrivals were living in poverty and destitution, and evangelical Christians duly offered them practical support while at the same time taking heed of the biblical injunction that the gospel should be preached "first to the Jew, then to the Gentile".

Ironically, in view of the holocaust they were later to suffer, it was a German called Joseph Frey who proposed the formalisation of this organisation as the London Society for the Promotion of Christianity Among the Jews, which won the support of a number of parliamentarians – in fact its supporters read like a Who's Who of England's most important people at the time.

It was meant to be cross-denominational but, when a funding crisis struck in 1817 and an appeal was made to the churches, it was the Anglicans who provided the cash, and it thus became an Anglican mission. CMJ's mission came out of a biblical understanding of the church's responsibility to the Jewish people along with the prophecies about their restoration to the Promised Land because, in the wake of the French Revolution, there was a sense of the world falling apart rather in the manner used to describe events leading up to the Second Coming of Christ. And evangelical Christians knew from their Bibles that the Jews would have to be back in their land before that could take place.

A man called Lewis Way, who was left a large sum of money to be used "for the glory of God", became a significant benefactor and advocate for the establishment of a Jewish homeland, a proposal which gained considerable political backing. CMJ duly established centres in Eastern Europe, Russia, the Middle East, Tehran and Morocco and by the mid-19th century was the biggest missionary organisation in the world with over 200 missionaries in the field.

"The heartbeat of CMJ has always been the sharing of the gospel with Jewish people," Robin explained from his office set in beautiful Nottinghamshire countryside. "And we are still very active in Israel."

It was in 1840 that they made the decisive move to establish themselves in 'Palestine' where, on behalf of the British Government, they set up a consulate in Jerusalem – the first European country to do so. They also wanted to build a church, but were initially refused because the territory was then part of the Turkish Ottoman Empire, where no Christian churches were allowed. But when they re-submitted their planning application as a "chapel for the consul and his wife to worship", they were granted permission for what became, in Robin's words, "the biggest chapel you've ever seen". Christ Church was duly consecrated in 1849 and is the oldest protestant church in the Middle East.

CMJ continued to work both politically and theologically to persuade the British Government to grant a Jewish homeland in Palestine, and the promise was eventually made in 1917 with Foreign Secretary Arthur James Balfour's declaration to that effect following the defeat of the Turks by General Allenby's forces in World War I.

Meanwhile CMJ established several centres in the territory while also building hospitals and schools and were thus highly influential in creating an infrastructure for the Jewish state. It also had the effect of provoking the Jews to do even better. For example, after rabbis threatened to ex-communicate patients treated at CMJ's hospital, the Jews responded by building their own, Haddasha, now one of the most famous hospitals in the world.

Eventually, in 1948, Israel was 'born again' as a nation in fulfilment of prophecy and – also in fulfilment of prophecy that they would come from the north, south, east and west – Jewish people began returning to their ancient homeland. "Now for the first time, there are more Jewish people in Israel than in any other country, just beating America at seven million," Robin told me in 2009.

But the restoration of Israel is seen in the Bible as a two-stage process: first the physical, then the spiritual. The first has taken place – though the process is by no means complete – and the second has begun, initially with a trickle, now something of a vibrant stream and soon, in God's perfect timing, to become a river. Such a spiritual re-birth will effectively become a reality when the nation as a whole recognises Jesus as their long-promised Messiah, when their hearts will be softened (Jeremiah, Ezekiel) and, with the returning Christ, they will "look upon him whom they have pierced" (Zechariah).

Many today scoff at the prospect, but actually we are already witnessing the greatest event since the coming of Christ as a babe in Bethlehem. For the return of the Jews to the Promised Land and their subsequent spiritual renewal will usher in the Second Coming of Jesus, so the Bible tells us!

"There are now more Jewish people coming to faith in Yeshua than at any time in history," said Robin, adding: "There is openness to Jesus which was most certainly not there even ten years ago."

Some of the first Messianic congregations met in CMJ centres – at Christ Church, Mt Carmel and Jaffa – and the movement took off after 1967, significantly following the re-unification of Jerusalem as a result of the Six-Day War, the first time the entire city had been under Jewish control for more than two thousand years!

This also coincided with the outbreak of the worldwide charismatic movement among the traditional churches which involved a renewed understanding and experience of the work of the Holy Spirit. "We're still fundamentally doing the same thing, which is sharing the gospel with Jewish people and using whatever resources at our disposal to do so," Robin added.

But CMJ – along with other Christian organisations working on behalf of the Jews – come under much opposition, both from Orthodox Jews and the Church. "You could feel almost friendless. The Orthodox Jews are sometimes violently antagonistic towards missionaries and the church as a whole doesn't understand ministry to the Jews anymore in terms of it being a priority or especially close to God's heart."

The latter problem is primarily due to so-called Replacement Theology, the belief that because the Jews as a whole rejected Jesus at his coming, the Old Testament promises applying to them have now been transferred to the Church as the 'new Israel'. "It has had a very powerful influence and originally came about back in 300 AD with the decision to separate Christianity from Judaism."

Robin believes it's a schizophrenic way of thinking because its proponents argue that while the ancient blessings now apply to the Church, the curses (for disobedience) still apply to Israel because of her rejection of Jesus. It's complete nonsense, of course, because the church is rooted in Judaism, the early church was entirely Jewish and, in any case, God promised that he would never forsake the descendants of Abraham.

Shockingly, replacement theology led to the diabolical view that the Jews, rather than the sins of the world, were specifically responsible for the crucifixion of Jesus. It thus served to foment anti-Semitism and in time led to the Holocaust.

Thankfully CMJ was birthed during the great evangelical awakening which opened eyes to a right understanding of God's purposes for the Jews. Robin believes that when the Church experiences a deeper dimension of the Holy Spirit, it is generally accompanied by a greater understanding of Israel. After all, Jesus said the Spirit would lead us into all truth!

An added complication now is the current political situation in the Middle East which sees Christians, perhaps not surprisingly, wishing to support those perceived as the downtrodden and dispossessed. And they readily imbibe the notion of a largely anti-Israel media that it is the Palestinians who fall into this category.

CMJ's mission statement is summed up by three Es – evangelism, encouragement of Messianic believers and educating the Church about its Jewish roots. "There is an increasing openness among church members to understand more, but not yet a huge movement among the leadership. There's still an enormous mountain to climb. But God can change people's hearts and minds in an instant."

God's ultimate purpose for the Jewish people is that they will be a blessing to the nations. "The fact that there are tens of thousands of Messianic Jewish people in Israel today has caused God to bless the people around her so there is a real work of the Holy Spirit taking place in countries like Egypt and Iran. And nearly all the Messianic congregations have a burden to share their faith with their Arab brothers. So there is this real peace process taking place with Jesus at the centre. Many of the Messianic congregations are in fact a mixture of Arabs and Jews worshipping together. At the same time there are also tens of thousands of Muslims coming to faith in the surrounding countries. After all, they are all Semitic people and the promises of God's favour apply to the descendants of Ishmael as well as Isaac."

The prophet Isaiah foretold of a future time when there would be a highway through Israel from Egypt to Assyria (Iraq) in which Arabs and Jews would become a blessing to one another. And Robin believes we are starting to see a fulfilment of this prophecy. "These are both difficult and challenging, but also exciting times," he said.

'Scales fell from our eyes'

Robin Aldridge is a former headteacher of a Nottingham primary school where he kept being invited to a Baptist church by a member of staff. He and his wife Sue eventually ran out of excuses and visited the church where he recalls an "uncanny feeling that the pastor knew everything about me and was preaching to me personally".

"That set us off on a journey in which I personally tried to think my way through to God but then, during a weekend event at Cliff College in the Peak District, I had an overwhelming experience of Jesus and it completely broke me."

Sue came to her own decision for Christ and they got baptised together in 1982. Then, during the 1991 Gulf War, Sue was very worried about the conflict between Iraq and Kuwait and asked the pastor if they could host a prayer meeting for the purpose. Many came and when they heard on the 9pm news that Iraq had fired scud missiles into Israel, Robin and Sue had a revelation. "At that moment the scales fell off from our eyes – that what that war was all about was Israel and the Jewish people – and God gave us a burden for Israel."

Sue meanwhile, a drama graduate, now uses her acting skills very effectively for the cause to help convey the truths they try to bring on their travels. In due course they got more involved with CMJ, who are also represented in America, Ireland, South Africa, Australia, Canada and Singapore.

CHAPTER 6

The stench of anti-Semitism

Anti-Semitism has its roots, tragically, in the Christian church which explains why Jews generally are so discouraged from having anything to do with 'Gentile' Christians. It dates back to the notion taken up by the early 'Church Fathers' that the Jews were responsible for killing Jesus. But while that may have been technically correct, it betrays a complete lack of understanding of the incarnation and atoning sacrifice of our Lord, by which I mean God taking on human flesh and the sacrificial death he willingly suffered in atoning (making us one with God through forgiveness) for our sins. So there is a sense in which we all, by our sin, put Jesus on the cross and really we have the Jews to thank for ensuring that the Messiah fulfilled the purpose of his coming, which was to reconcile us with God through his shed blood, as we remember with gladness in Holy Communion every week.

But poison soon spreads through the system and misinformation, whether theological or political, will influence minds to carry out the most evil deeds imaginable. As with current propaganda about the Jews inciting Islamic terrorists to vent their frustration by blowing up innocent victims, so the gangrene of false teaching spread through the early church until, by the time of the Crusades in the Middle Ages, Jews were regarded as fair game for torture and murder. No wonder the sign of the cross (used by the Crusaders) struck fear into Jewish hearts over succeeding centuries. The Crusades were undertaken to recover the Holy Land from the Muslims, but these 'Christians' obviously had no understanding of the place in God's heart for the Jews or of his plans to bring them back to their ancient homeland.

Meanwhile Spain has greatly benefited from the many Latin (or Sephardic) Jews who blessed that nation with their skill and enterprise and from whom I myself am descended. But 'apartheid' was practiced against them and hundreds of thousands were expelled for not converting to Christianity while others, including 50,000 who continued to practice their faith in secret, were burnt at the stake when their 'deceit' was uncovered during the infamous 15th century Spanish Inquisition.

Even Martin Luther, otherwise a hero of the Protestant Reformation, raged against the Jews to whom he referred as "poisonous envenomed worms", urging their synagogues to be set on fire, their homes destroyed, that they should be put under one roof or in a stable like gypsies 'to teach them they are not master in our land' and drafted into forced labour and made to earn their bread 'by the sweat of their noses'. Is it any wonder, with the influence he commanded, that these pernicious ideas helped to give rise – in his own land – to the most appalling atrocity ever committed against the Jewish people when six million were burned in Nazi ovens after being forced into their 'labour camps'? And in the 'light' of Luther's comment, it is chilling to note how the gypsies suffered with them. In *Mein Kampf*, the book in which he set out his plans for changing the world, nominally Catholic Hitler wrote that "by defending myself against the Jew, I am fighting for the work of the Lord".

It would be appropriate to mention at this point, however, that not everyone took Luther's – and subsequently Hitler's – line. Pastor Dietrich Bonhoeffer was among them, and he paid with his life. And then there was the Dutch Christian family of Corrie Ten Boom who risked their lives by hiding Jews in their apartment. They eventually got found out and were sent to a concentration camp where Corrie watched her sister die at the cruel hands of the Nazi captors and yet, by the grace of God, was later able to forgive the guard responsible when she met him at a Christian meeting.

And it is only the grace of God that is able to reconcile Jew and Gentile, Arab and Jew, Protestant and Catholic in Ireland and black and white in South Africa. It is a little-known fact that many of Hitler's leading henchmen repented of their connivance in his evil regime and turned to Christ as they awaited execution following the Nuremberg Trials of 1946. This remarkable episode in the annals of Christian heroism came about through an American military chaplain whose own son had been killed by the Germans in the war, but who nevertheless managed to overcome his reluctance to share the gospel with the enemy. He visited all those on trial in their prison cells and graciously introduced many of them to the Messiah of the very nation they had sought to destroy.

Wolves in sheep's clothing

They say that politicians do not learn from history. But the same is true for some sections of the church, sadly. The Methodists of Great Britain, who in 2010 voted to boycott Israeli goods emanating from the West Bank, should hang their heads in shame at the diabolical report they produced purporting to present a peaceful solution to millennia of conflict in the Middle East.

Withdraw from the 'occupied territories' and peace will result, they concluded without addressing the issue of why this did not happen following recent withdrawal from areas including the Gaza Strip. Like the anti-war socialists of pre-World War II France, who encouraged appeasement with Hitler, they evidently concluded that the Jews must have done something particularly heinous to have caused the fascist anti-Zionist groups in the Middle East to seek their destruction. So that, far from promoting the cause of peace, their recommendations will have only served to encourage Muslim efforts to destroy Israel and, in the process, potentially bring the entire world into a conflagration on the scale of Armageddon. Although entitled 'Justice for Palestine and Israel', the document actually endorses a dishonest and one-sided understanding of the conflict.

As expressions of anti-Semitism become increasingly prevalent throughout the world, particularly in Europe, the authors of this report clearly saw fit to fan the flames by portraying the Jewish state as the primary source of conflict in the Middle East, and the world. Not surprisingly, the report makes no mention of the role played by Haj-Amin al-Husseini, the Grand Mufti of Jerusalem, in the Holocaust. This man courted the Nazi regime in his effort to keep Jews from Palestine. And as a result of his relationship he recruited Bosnian Muslims to serve in Waffen SS units in 1943 – units that were responsible for the murder of Jews in Croatia and Hungary. In addition to blocking deals that would have saved Jewish children from the death camps, he also spread Nazi propaganda into the Middle East through radio broadcasts and leaflets. And this has no doubt had an enduring effect on the outlook of Muslim organisations.

And instead of acknowledging that the leaders of five Arab countries declared war on Israel and promised its destruction in 1948, the Methodist working group merely reported that in 1949 "several Arab countries attempted to intervene in support of the Palestinians". In addition, the claim that 750,000 Palestinian refugees were "forced from the country" is distorted because Arab leaders called on many of their people to leave Palestine to make way for Israel's destruction. And most tellingly, the report omits any mention of the failed negotiations that took place at Camp David in 2000 during which Yassir Arafat refused Ehud Barak's offer of a state comprising all of the Gaza Strip and most of the West Bank.

As writer Dexter Van Zile reports, "in order to make their story work, the authors of the Methodist report ignore Arab and Muslim misdeeds in the Middle East and the ideas that motivate them and focus almost exclusively on Israeli actions and their impact on Palestinians." They have fallen for the temptation that has become irresistible to many – that suicide terrorists must have had good reason to do something so desperate; that it must somehow be a rational response to real-life conditions. And yet the report fails to deal with the anti-Semitic ideologies used to justify violence against Israel and deny its right to exist.

And although, to their credit, they include a condemnation of replacement theology (the idea that the church has replaced Israel as far as God's promises are concerned), this is rendered meaningless by their failure to address the issues relating to Muslim teaching regarding the Jewish people, portraying them, for example, as the "enemies of God". And in any case the report calls on Methodists to embrace the Kairos Document issued in 2009 by Palestinian Christian leaders which was itself condemned as 'supersessionist' (another term for embracing replacement theology) and anti-Semitic by the Central Conference of American Rabbis.

The central theme of the report – that the key hindrance to security and lasting peace is the 'occupation' of Palestinian territory – is completely undermined by the plain fact that the very opposite has been true, that Israeli withdrawals have often been a precursor to increased violence. In fact Israel has been attacked from nearly every bit of territory from which it has withdrawn since the 1990s. After they withdrew their soldiers from towns and cities in the West Bank in the 1990s, these same areas became recruiting grounds for suicide bombers. After they withdrew from Lebanon in 2000, Hezbollah attacked Israel from this country six years later. And after Israel withdrew from Gaza in 2005, she was attacked by Hamas the following year.

As I have said, the question of so-called 'occupation' is one of the greatest deceptions put about by the media. A Palestinian line may be the political-ly-correct one, but it's not ultimately the right one! Methodists and other Christians should stop thinking in such a worldly way, as the scripture urges, and pray for wisdom and understanding from above.

A dangerous new alliance

Meanwhile an alarming new anti-Israel alliance has emerged between evangelical Christian leaders and radical Islamists. And I say this with trepidation and shame, because I count myself as evangelical, but cannot allow such a development to go unnoticed and end up being generally accepted.

As reported in an in-depth article in the Spectator magazine by the hugely-respected Daily Mail columnist Melanie Phillips, Anglican vicar and author Rev Stephen Sizer shared a platform at an anti-Israel meeting with an

Islamist called Ismail Patel, who has not only accused Israel of 'genocide' and 'war crimes' but considers Disney to be a Jewish plot and supports Hamas, Iran and Syria.

Sizer is a virulent opponent of so-called 'Christian Zionism' – the perfectly biblical belief that God's ancient promises to Israel, as recorded both in the Old and New Testaments, still apply. Such Christians pray, for example, that beleaguered Jews will continue to be protected until such time as they turn en masse to their Messiah, Jesus, when their spiritual eyes are opened. Meantime a growing number of so-called 'Messianic Jews' (both in Israel and abroad) have already recognised Yeshua (Jesus) in keeping with Bible predictions.

Others like Sizer, however, believe God has forsaken the Jews because of their initial rejection of their Messiah (forgetting that the early church was almost entirely Jewish) and that the Church inherits all her promises. This profound split among evangelicals has existed for some time but has now taken a dangerous turn. It also represents a huge inconsistency in the Church of England which has recently banned its clergy from joining the far-right BNP (British National Party), but is apparently happy to see them siding with the forces of Islamo-fascism. However, there is an even bigger issue at stake. And that is the whole business of political opposition to Israel in Britain and the West, now supported by leading churchmen.

Much-respected authority on Israel, Lance Lambert, has recently repeated a prophecy he gave in November 1998 relating to the Lord's furious anger with the nations who oppose Israel and who wish to divide her land and destroy her heritage. He said that God would judge these nations with a number of natural and other catastrophes and, particularly, with financial collapse. "...I will touch them where it will hurt them most," Lambert had prophesied, "for I will touch their power and the foundations of their affluence and prosperity. I will smash their prosperous economies, says the Lord."

How we as a nation, and as individuals, treat the Jews is fundamental to what we are, and what will become of us, according to the Bible. "I will bless those who bless you and whoever curses you I will curse," the Lord promised to Abraham. But leading churchmen have been co-ordinating a new approach to Islam which amounts to appeasement and at the same time are seeking to discredit those who warn against the Islamisation of Britain like Dr Patrick Sookhdeo and the former Bishop of Rochester, Michael Nazir-Ali.

"Extreme hostility towards Israel is the default position among bishops and archbishops..." says Melanie Phillips, who adds: "With Christians around the world suffering forced conversion, ethnic cleansing and murder at Islamist hands, the church utters not a word of protest."

She sees it as horrifying that so many in the church should be accommodating those who stand for the persecution of Christians, the destruction of

Western values and the genocide of the Jews, and said it seemed the church was truly supping with the devil "and setting the stage for a repeat of an ancient tragedy".

It is well to be reminded of the numerous promises God has made to Israel. Here is just one: "Only if these decrees vanish from my sight," declares the Lord, "will the descendants of Israel ever cease to be a nation before me." This is what the Lord says: "Only if the heavens can be measured and the foundations of the earth below be searched out will I reject all the descendants of Israel because of all they have done," declares the Lord. (Jeremiah 31:35-37)

After all, Jesus did pray as he was suffering excruciating pain on the cross: "Father, forgive them, for they know not what they do," reflecting the compassion of his ancestor Joseph who told his brothers who treated him so despicably by sending him into slavery: "It was not you who sent me here, but God."

Jesus warned that in the last days before his return false prophets would arise and deceive many, possibly including some of his own followers, and that many would turn away from the faith. It is not a pleasant task to have to confront fellow Christians in public, but there are times when it is both necessary and vital. We have false prophets in our midst whose message needs to be openly challenged, as the prophet Elijah did on Mt Carmel in ancient times. The 400 prophets of Baal at that time were leading Israel astray to worship foreign gods and idols, and Elijah saw it as his task to challenge them to a contest in which the God who answered by fire would be worshipped as God. Elijah successfully prayed down the fire and the nation turned back to God. This amazing event was something of a precursor to Pentecost, when the Church was born and when the fire of the Holy Spirit came down and brought unity, truth, purity and power to the message of the gospel. We need another Pentecost!

'Hitler' is still alive

The 70th anniversary of the outbreak of World War II was aptly remembered on the BBC Breakfast Show in 2009 with the re-enactment of the extraordinary rescue of 700 Jewish children from Prague by British diplomat Nicholas Winton.

The British Prime Minister Neville Chamberlain declared war on Germany on September 3 1939 after they refused to withdraw their troops from Poland following an invasion. The Allies entered the global war that followed, which claimed 50 million lives, in a bid to stop the cancerous spread of Nazism. The godless, fanatical and inhumane spirit that drove the National Socialists had already been clearly evident throughout the rise to power of Hitler during the thirties and, in particular, on the infamous night when Jewish businesses were attacked.

The Allies rightly responded to the Fuehrer's aggression, but too late to save six million Jews from a ghastly death in the concentration camps. True, Britain was still recovering from the shock and dreadful loss of life of World War I and was in no mood for another war. But Winston Churchill, who had been warning Parliament for years of the need to deal with Hitler, was eventually vindicated and, as an ageing but inspirational Premier, led Britain to victory in the six-year conflict.

The amazing foresight and compassion of Nicholas Winton, aged 100 at the time of the anniversary, saved all those precious children whose parents were sent to the gas chambers. We need more like him today, especially in politics and in the church, who can see what is happening and take action to do something about it.

For Jews worldwide, and especially in Israel itself, are in just as much danger today – perhaps more. It is worth remembering that in 1939 there was no Jewish state to which persecuted Jews could escape. The creation of the state at the behest of the United Nations in 1948 – a fulfilment of biblical promise but also of British Government assurances – was eventually facilitated through the worldwide sympathy generated by gruesome pictures of holocaust victims.

But now much of that is forgotten and the victim – in media eyes at least – has become the bully. Now Israel, taking up only a fraction of the land originally promised by political agreement (quite apart from holy writ), has become the 'occupier' accused of conducting 'apartheid' policies in discriminating against Palestinians.

Israel's politicians and military personnel are certainly not without fault. But the fact remains that Jews generally, and Israel in particular, are now in great danger of total extinction in much the same way as they were under Hitler. I personally don't believe it will happen because I trust the scriptures which say that once they return from all the nations to which they have been scattered, they will never again be removed.

But one has to be practical and note the rantings of a new Hitler on their doorstep, President Mahmoud Ahmadinejad of Iran, who has on several occasions declared his intention to "wipe Israel off the map".

Similar sentiments have been expressed for some time by terrorist groups like the PLO, Hezbollah and Hamas. And Iran, which has also been fanning the flames in Iraq, is expected to be capable of launching a nuclear weapon very soon.

The persecution of the Jews has a history going back millennia and is not easy to grasp. But it basically comes down to jealousy over a race especially chosen by God. Now that might seem like politically incorrect discrimination of the sort the EU would happily ban, but if our Creator chooses to have a favourite, who are we mere mortals to argue?

This does not, however, mean God has no love for other nations. On the contrary, he sent his only Son, the Jewish man Jesus, to die for the sins of all people and ultimately fulfil the biblical promise that the Jews would become a blessing to the entire world. It's time to stand up and be counted for the Jewish people. Because if you love Jesus (and 70% of Britons claim to be Christian), you should also love the Jews.

Jews fear another holocaust

So as Jews celebrate the feast of Purim each year, recalling the time they were saved from annihilation by the Persian king Xerxes through the intervention of Queen Esther, they are also waking up to the reality that, even in 'enlightened' 21st century Europe, another holocaust is possible – and perhaps inevitable.

An alarming rise in anti-Semitism has been reported throughout Europe, notably in France, but also in Britain – partly due to the current economic crisis as, just as was the case during the depression of the 1930s, Jews are being blamed for the situation. The depression in turn led to Hitler's holocaust and now, in a poll of Europeans, almost one-third blamed the Jews for the crisis.

As former Europe Minister and Labour MP Denis MacShane wrote in an article entitled *The writing is on the synagogue wall* published in The Times, there were reports of as many attacks on Jews – verbal, vandalism and some violent – in the first weeks of 2009 as in the first six months of the previous year.

"Attacks on Jews and Jewishness constitute the canary in the coal mine that tells us something is going seriously wrong," he wrote. "As the world enters a new era of crisis, anti-Semitism is back. History, as ever, begins to repeat itself."

Referring to the condemnation against Israel for Muslims killed in Gaza and elsewhere, he wondered why there was no outrage against the massacres of Muslims committed by their own people in different parts of the world so far this century. (Syria is a more recent example). Part of the answer, I believe, is the intense propaganda war against Israel conducted by the media.

A shocking example of media bias in Britain was the publication in the Sunday Times on Holocaust Memorial Day 2013 of a cartoon depicting Israel as committing genocide against the Palestinians, suggesting of course that the Jewish nation had taken a lead from their Nazi persecutors. I'm glad to say that the paper subsequently apologised profusely, describing it as a "terrible mistake". But it should never have slipped through the editorial 'net' in the first place.

Baroness Deech had urged the House of Lords "not to believe all that they read in the newspapers about damage and killings in Gaza. We do not have the evidence."

But what we do now know is that casualty figures were grossly exaggerated – for example, an Italian reporter, citing hospital sources, said that 600 at the most had died, whereas the official figure was 1,300. And Yvonne Green, a British writer, discovered on visiting Gaza herself that many of the incidents reported during the war had been totally fabricated. There was no evidence, for example, of indiscriminate devastation – the Israelis had made precision attacks on Hamas' infrastructure. And empty hospital beds signified a story very different to the lies the mainstream media had drip-fed into the minds and hearts of a public only hearing one side of the story.

"Terrorised Gazans used doublespeak when they told me most of the alleged 5,500 wounded were being treated in Egypt and Jordan," Yvonne Green reported on-line in the Jerusalem Post. "They want it known that the figure is a lie, and showed me that the wounded weren't in Gaza. No evidence exists of their presence in foreign hospitals, or of how they might have got there. From the mansions of the Abu Ayida family at Jebala Rayes to Tallel Howa (Gaza City's most densely populated residential area), Gazans contradicted allegations that Israel had murderously attacked civilians. They told me again and again that both civilians and Hamas fighters had evacuated safely from areas of Hamas activity in response to Israeli telephone calls, leaflets and megaphone warnings."

In addition, she found the UN-run school allegedly hit by Israeli shells visibly intact! And yet, to add fuel to the flames of anti-Jewish feeling, we had the spectacle of an Israel-bashing nationwide tour in 'Solidarity with Gaza' culminating outside the G20 meetings in London. And America, Israel's long-time friend, is now set to pressure them into dividing Jerusalem, and giving away Judea and Samaria – when the Bible warns of dire consequences for anyone who tries to divide the land God has promised to his people.

Determined to avert such a disaster is Mike Evans of the Jerusalem Prayer Team – a Christian movement pledged to defend the Jewish people – who says that if the American plan succeeds, East Jerusalem, where Jesus was crucified and raised, will become an Islamic fundamentalist capital where neither Jews nor Christians will be welcome. And he adds: "If Israel is forced to kow-tow, America is doomed. Jerusalem's title deed belongs to God Almighty. Heaven and earth met in Jerusalem and will meet again."

And he reminds us of God's promise to Abraham: "I will bless them that bless thee, and curse him who curses thee." Alarmingly, the highly respected American preacher David Wilkerson prophesied shortly before his untimely death in a car crash that the United States was about to experience a great calamity! He did the same in advance of 9/11 and was proved right!

Iranians protest as Israel quakes

Meanwhile a counter-revolution has been building up in Iran involving up to half-a-million students and others taking to the streets in protest at the harshness of its regime more than three decades after the Islamic revolution swept the Shah from power. And it is no coincidence, I'm sure, that it comes at the same time as reports of many in the country forsaking Islam for Christianity, an offence punishable by death.

But Iranians would do well to reflect on the injustice suffered by Israelis, who have had to endure repeated rocket fire along with threats of annihilation from Iranian leaders as well as terrorist groups they sponsor like Hamas and Hezbollah. The whole scenario serves to highlight the point Israeli Prime Minister Benjamin Netanyahu made to President Obama: that the issue of Iran must be dealt with before there can be peace with the Palestinians. This is because Iran supplies arms to the Palestinian leaders (Hamas) and both are committed to the destruction of Israel.

What is the point of a 'two-state solution' which creates a perfect platform right on your doorstep for terrorists who are determined to "wipe Israel off the map"? It's true Mr Netanyahu has apparently made concessions which indicate a softening in his approach towards the idea of such a solution. But he is all too aware that Iran continues openly to enrich uranium under the pretext of building nuclear power plants, with China deeply involved and North Korea supplying them with long-range missiles.

Meanwhile Israel is coming under great pressure to accept East Jerusalem as the capital of a Palestinian state which virtually amounts to giving away its 'soul'. For more than 60 years (and several millennia in terms of Jewish history), Jerusalem has formed the nucleus of Israel's national identity and cohesion.

The Iranian protestors, and all who sympathise with them, can look forward to a time of worldwide justice when, according to the Bible, Jesus Christ will return to reign on earth from Jerusalem – with equity and absolute fairness. "He will bring justice to the nations. He will not shout or cry out, or raise his voice in the streets. A bruised reed he will not break, and a smouldering wick he will not snuff out. In faithfulness he will bring forth justice; he will not falter or be discouraged till he establishes justice on earth. In his law the islands will put their hope." (Isaiah 42)

Unfortunately such a scenario will only come about after a terrible conflagration in the Middle East – something that appears to be coming to a climax right now. But the 'Prince of Peace' will reign in the end.

The rise of anti-Semitism in Europe is very worrying, and proof indeed that we rarely learn from our past mistakes, especially with the Holocaust now fading into the pages of history. The situation in France is particularly dire, with many attacks on Jews reported, and with this in mind the BBC's *Who Do You Think You Are?* series on the family trees of the famous was both poignant and disturbing.

Newscaster Davina McCall was very moved by the discovery that her maternal great-grandfather was the French police chief who spoke up for Richard Dreyfus in the notorious case at the dawn of the 20th century which saw the latter – a Jewish army officer – wrongly accused of treason for allegedly passing on military secrets to the Germans. He was eventually pardoned – thanks in part to the intervention of Hennion (Davina's ancestor), derided as a 'Jew-lover' – when it became obvious from a worldwide outcry that it was all part of anti-Jewish feeling. Too many, I'm afraid, are more apt to repeat the errors of their forefathers than their courageous acts of selfless love to which we should all aspire.

From the same country came much more recent reports of a horrifying catalogue of anti-Semitic violence which included the firebombing of Jewish religious centres in Montpellier, Strasbourg and Marseilles, a car being set on fire after ramming into a synagogue in Lyon and a Jewish sports club in Toulouse being attacked with Molotov cocktails. "Will the world say nothing again, as it did in Hitler's time?" was the despairing cry, adding that police in Paris had reported up to a dozen anti-Jewish incidents a day over the previous 30 days including walls being defaced with slogans like 'Death to the Jews' and a gunman opening fire on a kosher butcher's shop in Toulouse.

CHAPTER 7

The Battle for Israel

Amidst all the arguments for and against God now raging in Western society, perhaps the best in his defence is the existence and survival against all odds of Israel. All the hordes of hell have stood against the tiny nation determined to wipe her from the face of the earth. But no plot to destroy God's chosen people has ever succeeded. From the plan of Haman at the time of Queen Esther thousands of years ago to Hitler's 'final solution' in the 20th century, they have all failed miserably despite the devastation and bloodshed caused in the process.

And even after a window of compassion following the holocaust paved the way for the re-establishment of a Jewish homeland, she was attacked from all sides by implacable Arab opponents determined to stop her progress – and yet in just six days (in 1967), she fought off her enemies. This is plainly because, in the words of former Muslim fundamentalist Dr Daniel Shahesteh, "God chose Israel and set her aside for himself in order to fulfil his eternal plan for the nations through her…"

"Amazingly," he wrote in an article for 'Israel and Christians Today', "the enemies of Israel have been trying to destroy her for thousands of years. Yet she still survives! By no means has God rejected Israel. He has a covenant with her, and in the end he will send his deliverer to Zion to save her from her sins and enemies."

Dr Shahesteh was astonished after reading Psalm 83 for the first time. A passage from this psalm reads thus: "'Come,' they say, 'let us destroy them as a nation, that the name of Israel be remembered no more.'

With one mind they plot together; they form an alliance against you…"

The activists involved in the Gaza aid flotilla debacle violently confronted Israel's Navy, chanting battle cries invoking the killing of Jews and calling for martyrdom, forcing the military to defend themselves. But in revealing the true nature of Islam, an Arabic former Muslim lady writes in the same newspaper of the spirit of hatred and deception that permeates the religion: "While they are telling the world Islam is a religion of peace, they still want to continue with the Jihad (holy war) against non-Muslim countries. While one leader says 'Let's kill all the Jews and take over Rome', another says to Western media that Islam is a religion of peace and that they are deeply offended by the anti-Islam rhetoric. To play this sick game, Muslim culture must live a dysfunctional double life where everyone is deceived, including Muslims," she adds.

One of the greatest deceptions put about by the Western media is over the land of Israel itself, including the area known as the 'Occupied Territories' which in fact legally belong to her. An agreement was reached in April 1920 at a conference called by the League of Nations at San Remo where the (British Government's) Balfour Declaration of 1917 – granting a homeland for the Jews far more extensive than that they currently occupy – was recognised and incorporated into international law.

This undermines virtually all the pronouncements of politicians pontificating about the 'rights' of the Palestinians because the reality of the situation is that the 'West Bank' and Gaza are not in fact an illegal 'occupation', but part of the land originally assigned as the state of Israel. Come on politicians! Do your homework. The trouble is that U.S. President Obama's 20-year membership of a church led by Rev Jeremiah Wright, with his actively pro-Palestinian position, has been the breeding ground for an anti-Israel attitude. The pro-Palestinian line may be politically-correct, but it's not ultimately the right one!

Israel's re-birth as a nation was almost aborted at the very start when, immediately following the declaration of the new state as agreed by the United Nations, they came under attack from all sides by neighbouring Arab countries unwilling to welcome or recognise them. This was only the first of a succession of wars centred on Israel's right to the land, from which they have survived by what can surely only be attributed to miraculous intervention.

In 1967 this tiny, fledgling nation saw off her enemies in just six days and recovered territory lost in the 1948 war of independence which saw Jordan annex East Jerusalem (the Old City) and the so-called West Bank (Judea and Samaria). So it was that in 1967 the Old City of Jerusalem – regarded as the focal point of Judaism, a holy place of great significance – came into Israeli hands for the first time in more than 2,000 years and was understandably the cause of much rejoicing.

The Yom Kippur War of 1973, however, lasted four months and was quite a different matter in which the now 25-year-old state came close to annihilation. It involved the biggest and most ferocious tank battles in history and Israel was hugely outnumbered both in men and arms. Yet just when the enemies from Syria and Egypt could have overwhelmed their victims, they inexplicably halted their advance, allowing Israel to re-group. Jordan, thankfully, did not enter the war, which was quite possibly another factor contributing to Israel's survival.

It has to be said that Christians were engaged in serious intercessory prayer during the war, which no doubt had something to do with these 'miraculous' outcomes. But most shocking of all was that this premeditated attack deliberately designed to catch Israel unawares was launched on the Day of Atonement (Yom Kippur), a sacred day of prayer and fasting when all business stops and even soldiers would be resting or on leave in honour of the God who forgave their sins. And it could have led to World War III or possibly even Armageddon – a terrible future conflict described in the Book of Revelation when many nations would come against Israel. The reason Syria and Egypt were so well equipped was because the Soviet Union supplied them with weapons and, when a Russian warship was dispatched to Alexandria armed with ballistic missiles containing nuclear warheads, President Nixon – fortunately not too distracted by his domestic problems over the 'Watergate' break-in scandal – declared an international American military alert for the first time since the Cuban crisis of 1962. As a result, the ship sailed back to the Black Sea and a possible holocaust was narrowly averted.

The Arab Spring

So how will Israel be affected by the so-called Arab Spring – the popular push for freedom and democracy across the Middle East? Highly regarded American journalist David Dolan, who has been based in Israel for the past three decades, says it should more correctly be labelled an Islamic Revolution which poses great dangers for Israel, until now the only real democracy in that area. Dolan, who has twice been mugged and once shot at while visiting his home country, suggesting that living in the Holy Land is safer than some American cities, says that Coptic Christians formed a significant percentage of the original demonstrations in Egypt, but that it wasn't long before the more organised Muslim Brotherhood took over the movement so that, whereas they were formerly ruled by a despot, they were now "facing the mob" with Christians being murdered as they come under increasing attack from fundamentalist Muslims. In Bahrain, meanwhile, a relatively benign regime fairly friendly both to the West and Israel, the uprising has been led by Shi-ites from Lebanon sent down from Hezbollah on behalf of Iran. But the U.S. 5th Fleet is based there and apparently told President Obama that they must not allow an uprising to succeed there.

Further complicating the scene is the confusing spectre of a U.S. President claiming to be a Christian despite having a Muslim father, a pretty untenable position in the Islamic world where such a choice would be regarded as betrayal. Dolan adds that an authoritative source had told him that, in going after Saddam Hussein in Iraq, America was focusing on the wrong thing. "You're going after the mouse and if you get rid of him you'll set 'the rat' free," the source had said, referring to Hezbollah and its backers, Syria and Iran. Syria, on Israel's northern borders and now in the midst of a bloody civil war, had the world's fourth biggest standing army and a massive chemical weapons arsenal, thanks to being a key Soviet ally. And its leader, Assad, is one of the most brutal rulers on earth who wouldn't think twice about mowing down his own people, which made it particularly difficult to deal with the threat it poses to the region.

So it is hardly surprising that Israel's military remains on very high alert with the belief that they are on the verge of a major surprise attack, such as happened at the start of the Yom Kippur War in 1973. Dolan adds that an ancient biblical prophecy that Damascus, Syria's capital, would one day be completely destroyed, could soon be fulfilled, as Hezbollah have already threatened a nuclear attack on Israel. And though Israel's leaders have insisted that they won't be the first to use weapons of mass destruction, they warn that they *will* be the second if attacked. And the aforementioned prophecy describes something akin to a nuclear strike! The logistical scenario is that tiny Israel (the size of Wales), with a population of seven million, is surrounded by four hostile Arab countries with a combined population of over 100 million. But the final battle in world history will be over Jerusalem where, if the Palestinians get their way, 350,000 Jews will be forced out of their homes! And that, says Dolan, is a highly unlikely outcome. He is confident, however, that "Iran is not going to destroy Israel" and that "the only solution for all people living in Jerusalem is a right relationship with (God) the Father."

And in this final battle, predicts the prophet Zechariah, Jerusalem would become "an immovable rock for all the nations" and all who tried to move it would injure themselves. (Zech 12.3) The city and its inhabitants would be protected so that even the feeblest among them would be "like David", and God would set out to destroy all the nations that attack her. This scenario rather neatly mirrors another extraordinary battle in which a young boy not old enough to join his brothers on the frontline pits himself against the Philistine giant Goliath, trusting in the Lord rather than mighty weapons, and slays him with just one stone accurately aimed at his forehead.

CHAPTER 8

Occupation, occupation, occupation

Let's get one thing straight before we go any further – Israel does not illegally occupy any territory. That might fly in the face of all the Western media reports you have heard or read, but it's the truth. A 1920 League of Nations law, which is still in force, gives Israel the legal right to Judea, Samaria (the West Bank), East Jerusalem and Gaza – now disputed territory claimed by the Palestinian Authority which is currently seeking recognition as a nation state by the UN, circumventing the 'peace process' of further negotiations with the Israelis and instead banking on growing worldwide support both from Arab countries and Western nations increasingly sympathetic to their cause.

But a biased media, along with Arab intimidation and pressure, and politicians with an agenda, have succeeded in turning all that upside down even to the extent of claiming that Israel itself has no historical connection with the Middle East area they currently occupy. Yet in fact it was at a 1920 conference at the Castello Devachan villa, overlooking the Italian Riviera town of San Remo, that agreements were made about Israel's future by the newly-formed League of Nations that are still legal today. And in doing so they were validating a declared policy of Britain who, in 1917, issued what became known as the Balfour Declaration, when Parliament agreed to the contents of a letter sent from Foreign Secretary Arthur James Balfour to Baron Rothschild, a leader of the British Jewish community, for transmission to the Zionist Federation of Great Britain and Ireland. It stated that *"His Majesty's government view with favour the establishment in Palestine of a national home for the Jewish people, and will use their best endeavours to facilitate the achievement of this object, it being clearly understood that nothing shall be done which may prejudice the civil and religious rights of existing non-Jewish communities in Palestine, or the rights and political status enjoyed by Jews in any other country."* The declaration was later incorporated into the peace treaty with Turkey and the Mandate for Palestine.

The province of Palestine was at the time still part of the Turkish Ottoman Empire, with whom Britain and her allies were at war. Yet within weeks Britain had liberated Palestine from Turkish rule through the efforts of General Allenby – a committed Christian who clearly understood God's purposes for the Jews – who led a bloodless victory through the use of bi-planes dropping leaflets on the population persuading them to surrender peacefully. This remarkable feat was surely prophesied thousands of years earlier by Isaiah when he wrote: "Like birds hovering overhead, the Lord Almighty will shield Jerusalem; he will shield it and deliver it, he will 'pass over' it and will rescue it." (Isaiah 31.5) Interestingly, the passage begins with a warning against those who rely on Egypt for their help – the reference to Egypt is often used in the Scriptures as a symbol of reliance on 'the flesh' (i.e. human help in the form of soldiers and ammunition) rather than seeking God's intervention, of which the amazing deliverance from the Turks is a shining example. Anyway, this phenomenal occurrence, which liberated Palestine from 1,800 years of colonial rule, meant Britain was now in a position to implement its policy on behalf of the Jews. I would also suggest that the World War in question going the way of the Allies (in 1917) was not entirely unconnected with Britain's avowed support for the Jews at this time.

The San Remo Conference was made up of the Allied Supreme Council attended by the four principal Allied powers of World War I represented by the Prime Ministers of Britain (David Lloyd George), France and Italy along with the Japanese ambassador Keishiro Matsui. And in accordance with the suggestion of American President Woodrow Wilson, the victorious allies had agreed not to acquire new colonies in the Middle East following the collapse of the Ottoman Empire, but rather establish new sovereign states. And because they recognised that not all areas of the Middle East were yet ready for full independence, they agreed to set up mandates for each territory with the respective powers in charge of implementing each one.

Mandates were agreed for Lebanon, Syria, Mesopotamia (Iraq) and Palestine. But in the first three cases it was recognised that the indigenous people were able to govern themselves, with the mandatory power assisting in setting up the institutions of government where necessary. With Palestine, however, it was different because it was to become a homeland for the Jewish people, most of whom were not yet living in the land. Britain was to help Jewish immigrants prepare for the time when they could form a viable nation.

The Balfour Declaration was thus recognised and incorporated into international law with sovereignty over Palestine vested in the Jewish people in light of their historical connection to the land. And such entitlement could not be revoked unless its subjects chose to do so. The Arabs, meanwhile, gained equivalent rights in Lebanon, Syria and Mesopotamia. And the San Remo Agreement was included in the Treaty of Sevres and confirmed by the League of Nations council on July 24 1922 when all 51 nations voted in favour.

The Jewish state thus draws its legal existence from San Remo and not from the UN Partition Plan of 1947 (Resolution 181). Although the exact boundaries covered by the mandate were not defined, it was generally recognised as a vast area largely reflecting Israel's borders in biblical times and was extended to include Trans-Jordan (now known as Jordan) which subsequently (in 1946) gained its independence from Britain. But since there have been no other modifications to the mandate, its provisions are still applicable to all the land of Palestine west of the Jordan River, including what is now referred to as the West Bank and Gaza Strip.

And so when the State of Israel was formed in 1948, it was the fulfilment of the mandate, which had been created for this purpose, although the manner by which it came about left much to be desired with Britain terminating its role in 1947. The UN, which was formed after World War II and inherited all the agreements made by its predecessor, then proposed a Partition Plan, recommending the setting up of an Arab state, a Jewish state and an international zone to include Jerusalem. But this resolution (181) was only a recommendation, not an injunction. And though accepted by the Jewish leadership, it was rejected by the Arabs, and has no legal validity. Nevertheless, the 'two-state solution' much talked about by political leaders today was effectively implemented all those years ago when Jordan was created to absorb the area's Arab population. Why must a state already divided once be carved up yet again?

Though the UN accepted Israel into membership almost a year after its re-birth, it was only after she had managed to survive the war against her which immediately followed independence when five surrounding Arab nations invaded the new state. Israel lost some of her territory – the Golan Heights to Syria, Judea and Samaria (including East Jerusalem) to Trans-Jordan, and the Gaza Strip to Egypt. But this acquisition of territory was illegal under international law (it is universally accepted that it is inadmissible to gain land by attacking another country).

As for Jordan's annexation of the 'West Bank', it was only recognised by two countries – Britain and Pakistan. Israel subsequently recaptured the territories she had lost in the Six Day War of June 1967 – another conflict forced upon her by the aggression of the surrounding nations. And, after all, they belonged to Israel anyway as the fulfilment of the mandate for Palestine. Israel has since (in 2005) withdrawn from the Gaza Strip, where 6,000 Jews had made their homes, in response to international pressure. But legally it remains part of Israel.

And so it should be obvious that the expression 'illegally occupied territory' with reference to Israel's presence, for example, in Judea and Samaria, is wholly inapplicable. A state cannot 'illegally occupy' its own territory. And Israel's legal entitlement to these lands confirms the Word of God on the issue for those of us who believe the Bible. In any case, Israel's withdrawal from the Gaza Strip has not led to peace, as they had been persuaded would be the case, but has created a mini-terror state that has repeatedly attacked her with thousands of rockets. And most Israelis believe the same thing would happen on an even bigger scale if Israel abandoned Judea and Samaria.

What's more, there is an extraordinary paradox in all this in that Christmas is a time when tens of millions around the world celebrate the birth of Jesus in Bethlehem, Judea, a location supposedly not now Jewish – and yet, as a Rabbi pointed out recently, the festival surely gives retroactive approval to a Jewish settlement on the West Bank dating back more than 2,000 years! The West Bank is actually the heart of the nation, containing 80% of the 'mountains of Israel' to which the Jewish people are prophesied to return.

CHAPTER 9

The Holocaust – lest we forget

Proof if ever it was needed that the Jews are the chosen race comes with the long list of Nobel Prizes achieved by them, especially when compared with those won by Muslims, as Spanish writer Sebastian Vilar Rodriguez did in an article published in 2008. He found that whereas Muslims, who represent 1,200 million people (20% of the world's population), could only count seven such prizes, the Jews – with a global population of 14 million (not much more than one per cent of their Islamic brothers) – could boast 129 of them for every sphere from literature, peace, physics and economics to medicine.

The writer was particularly reflecting on the holocaust, saying: "Europe died in Auschwitz… we killed six million Jews and replaced them with 20 million Muslims. In Auschwitz we burned a culture, thought, creativity and talent. We destroyed the chosen people, truly chosen, because they produced great and wonderful people who changed the world."

He said Muslims had brought religious extremism and death by blowing up trains (a reference to the Madrid bombings committed by Al Qaeda) whereas the Jews Europe had murdered had pursued nothing but life and peace. "The Jews do not promote the brainwashing of children in military training camps, neither do they hijack planes, kill Olympic athletes or blow themselves up in German restaurants. And there is not a single Jew who has destroyed a church. Nor have their leaders called for Jihad and death to Infidels (non-believers)."

Rodriguez did not have the benefit of foresight at the time he was writing to know that, within three years, Europe would be on the brink of complete economic collapse. But God's ancient promise to Abraham still applies, that those who bless the Jews will themselves be blessed while those who curse them will come under judgment. Cornelius was a Roman centurion mentioned in the New Testament (Acts of the Apostles) who, though an officer of the occupying forces, was described as a devout and God-fearing man who gave generously to the poor and prayed to God regularly. He could well have been the same man mentioned in Luke's gospel whom Jesus commended for his tremendous faith and who cared for the Jews enough to build a synagogue for them. He then sent for their Messiah to heal his servant without insisting that he came under his roof as he believed he was unworthy of such an honour!

In the end Cornelius (and all those with him) were the means by which the entire Gentile world was blessed when they received the Holy Spirit, just as the disciples had done on the Day of Pentecost, through the preaching of the Apostle Peter who had risked his reputation by breaking with Jewish tradition in a very serious way in visiting this Gentile. But it turned into a breakthrough with tens of millions later benefiting from the faith, devotion and generosity of this Roman soldier as Peter and the rest of the apostles realised that Jesus was not for Jews only, but also for Gentiles!

In this context, the graph of Britain's rise and fall as a world power closely parallels its support or otherwise for the Jews. Our influence, for example, spread rapidly across the globe following the rise of giants like John Wesley and William Wilberforce who encouraged the British government to support a return of the Jews to their ancient homeland. And when this was made possible with the liberation of Jerusalem from the Turks by the godly General Allenby in 1917, the door was open for Britain to complete her God-given role.

But it took another world war, and the extermination of more than half Europe's Jews, before they were finally dragged kicking and screaming into playing their part as a helper of Israel. And though we had won two wars, the sun was fast sinking on our empire until virtually all vestiges of our great Judeo-Christian legacy had disappeared from view in a politically-correct atheist fog. Europe, meanwhile, is in financial meltdown with Britain – blessed by having the English Channel to separate them from their Continental cousins – splashing around in a desperate effort to keep their heads above water as the world faces the abyss. Would that we had been more prepared to stand for truth, integrity, for God and his people!

The spectre of another holocaust

Threatened with annihilation a couple of generations ago, the Jews still face another Holocaust. Iran, for one, has repeatedly stated through its president, Mahmoud Ahmadinejad, that it wants to see Israel "wiped off the map" while the terrorist organisations it supports – Hezbollah and Hamas – have similarly vowed to drive the nation into the sea.

With anti-Semitism on the rise throughout Europe and beyond, Holocaust Memorial Day is still marked in Britain at least – lest we forget. And this was the motive behind the action taken by former U.S. President Eisenhower when, as Supreme Commander of the Allied Forces at the end of World War II, he came across the horror of Hitler's death camps and insisted that photographs be taken – so that future generations would not be tempted to deny that such things happened as many, including the Iranian leader, have since done.

In fact the general apparently ordered all possible photographs to be taken, and that the German people from surrounding villages be ushered through the camps and even made to bury the dead. His reasoning effectively amounted to this: "Get it all on record now – get the films, the witnesses, because somewhere down the road of history some b****** will get up and say that this never happened."

The UK has recently debated whether to remove the Holocaust from its school curriculum because it 'offends' the Muslim population, some of whom claim it never occurred. It has not been removed as yet. But this is a frightening portent of the fear gripping the world and of how easily each country is succumbing to it. It is now 68 years since end of the war in Europe in which six million Jews along with millions of Christians, Russians and 1,900 Catholic priests were murdered, raped, burned, starved, beaten, experimented on and humiliated while the German people looked the other way! Now more than ever, with Iran, among others, claiming the Holocaust to be a myth, it is imperative to ensure the world never forgets. As someone has said, how many years will it be before the 9/11 attacks on the World Trade Centre 'never happened' because it offends Muslims in the U.S.

Meanwhile the Dutchwoman who helped protect the legendary Anne Frank and her family from the Nazis during World War II recently died, aged 100. Miep Gies was the last survivor of those who supplied food to young Anne, her parents, sister and four other Jews for two years before they were finally discovered and taken to a concentration camp.

According to a spokesperson for the Anne Frank House Museum in Amsterdam, Mrs Gies died of a neck injury following a fall at her home. Anne's diary, which chronicles her life in hiding from June 1942 to August 1944, was rescued by Mrs Gies. Anne died in Belsen concentration camp in March 1945, aged just 15, and Mrs Gies gave the diary to her father Otto, the family's only survivor, who published it in 1947. It was subsequently translated into 70 languages, and has been read by millions worldwide. The moving story of a young girl's extreme courage, optimism, humour and zest for life amidst great danger, it has also been seen on stage and screen, and is a stark reminder of the ever-present threat of anti-Semitism, and all the gross atrocities of which it is capable.

Even now Iran is building nuclear weapons with the intention of committing genocide against the Jews, with all the repercussions that will have for further conflagration in the Middle East. That's why we must never forget, nor let our children forget…

The apocalypse is now!

You don't need to go to the movies these days to be transported into an apparently unreal world of apocalyptic events. You just have to witness the world around you to know that you are indeed experiencing Apocalypse Now – for real!

Following the news just a few years ago that Iran (on the verge of producing a nuclear weapon) had test-fired missiles capable of a range of 1,200 miles – easily enough to reach its sworn enemy Israel – we heard of three mighty earthquakes within the space of just a few days, two in the Indonesian island of Sumatra and another thousands of miles away around the Pacific island of Samoa where an oceanic 'quake triggered a tsunami – all three leaving death and destruction in their wake.

One expert said it was extremely unusual for just two earthquakes to strike at the same time – and so far apart. But Jesus Christ predicted an increase of natural disasters, especially earthquakes, in the time immediately preceding his coming again. "There will be famines and earthquakes in various places… the beginning of birth-pains," he said, indicating a rise both in severity and in frequency of such events. And he added: "…nations will be in anguish and perplexity at the roaring and tossing of the sea. Men will faint from terror, apprehensive of what is coming on the world…"

In the same week, at the United Nations, the world was left standing in the 'valley of decision' (a biblical phrase) over whether to support terrorism on the one hand or much-maligned Israel on the other. "Either you support Israel or you support the terrorists," stated Israeli Prime Minister Benjamin Netanyahu, challenging world leaders to make up their mind after Iranian President Mahmoud Ahmadinejad was given a platform to address the nations, having repeatedly called for Israel to be "wiped off the map" and only days before having again insisted that the Holocaust was a myth exploited by 'Zionist criminals' to manipulate the world into accepting Israel's existence. In his New York speech, he once more assailed Israel, accusing the 'Zionist entity' of genocide in Gaza and of racism against Palestinian Arabs.

It was the following day that Mr Netanyahu responded, complete with dramatic proofs of the tragic reality of the Holocaust. He displayed the original blueprints for the construction of the Auschwitz-Birkenau death camps, signed by Hitler's deputy Heinrich Himmler. He also held up the original protocol of the infamous Wannsee Conference where the Nazi leadership

officially decided to implement the 'Final Solution' whose aim was to extermi-
nate the eleven million Jews then residing in Europe.

"Is this all a lie?" Mr Netanyahu pointedly asked world leaders, commend-
ing those countries that had decided to walk out on Ahmadinejad while scorn-
ing those who stayed to listen to and even applaud his tirade. The International
Christian Embassy in Jerusalem sent their wholehearted congratulations to
the Israeli leader for his powerful message and moral challenge. "In standing
up as he did, with such courage and strength of character, it was actually a
stand for decent people of goodwill everywhere," the embassy stated, adding
that the anti-Semitism expressed by the Iranian leader was unfortunately
finding acceptance even in 'polite' Western society.

More than six million Jews were brutally murdered by the Nazi regime.
Don't let history repeat itself. It's time to decide whether you support terrorism
or the Jews, who gave us Jesus, the Saviour of the world!

Being willing to pay the ultimate price

Some soldiers won the Victoria Cross posthumously, but no recipient of
the newly introduced Elizabeth Cross instituted by our Queen will know
about the recognition won for their bravery as it is for those who pay the
ultimate price in battle. It was poignant and powerful that, speaking of the
award, former army chief Sir Richard Dannatt told the BBC Songs of Praise
programme of the appropriateness of the medal taking the form of a cross,
the ultimate meaning of which was that it was where Jesus Christ died in our
place for our sins.

On the subject of courage, my attention has of late been drawn to the
extraordinary work of Irena Sendler, who risked her life to save 2,500 Jewish
children from the Warsaw Ghetto, the punishment for which (if it had been
discovered) would have been almost certain death at the hands of the Nazis.
This Polish Catholic woman, who died recently aged 98, had obviously been
influenced by her compassionate doctor father, who perhaps paid the ultimate
price by defying anti-Semitic tendencies in treating poor Jewish patients
afflicted with typhoid fever as he died from the disease himself when Irena
was just nine years old.

Disguised as a nurse, Irena smuggled the children to safe hiding places
where she found non-Jewish families to adopt them but kept their true
identities in a jar she hid in a neighbour's garden. Her achievement went
largely unnoticed for many years until, in 2000, her story was uncovered by
four young students at a Kansas school, who won the state national history day
competition by writing a play, *Life in a Jar*, about Irena's heroism.

Irena was greatly influenced by her father and was a social worker when Germany invaded Poland in 1939. The pivotal influence on her life was something her parents had drummed into her. "I was taught that if you see a person drowning, you must jump into the water to save them, whether or not you can swim," she said.

And so, appalled by conditions in the ghetto to which Jews were herded, Irena plunged in by joining Zegota, the Council for Aid to Jews organised by the Polish underground resistance movement.

She delivered food, medicine and clothing but, because so many were dying of starvation and disease, she decided to help the Jewish children escape. Persuading parents to part with their children was in itself an awful task, and neither was it easy to find families willing to shelter them. But, wearing a star armband as a sign of her solidarity with Jews, she began smuggling them out in various ways – in an ambulance, coffins, body bags, potato sacks and even a mechanic's tool box. In the end she rescued more than twice as many Jews as German industrialist Oskar Schindler who sheltered 1,200 of his Jewish workers and whose courage was depicted in the 1993 film *Schindler's List*. Irena achieved her goals with the active assistance of the church. "I sent most of the children to religious establishments," she recalled. "I knew I could count on the Sisters."

But the Nazis became aware of her activities and she was arrested, imprisoned and tortured by the Gestapo, who broke her feet and legs. But no-one could break her spirit as she refused to betray either her associates or any of the Jewish children in hiding. After the war she dug up the jars and tracked down the children she placed with adoptive families, but most had lost their original families in the Holocaust. Nominated for the Nobel Peace Prize in 2007, Irena did not think of herself as a hero, claiming no credit for her actions. "I could have done more," she said. She has, however, been honoured by international Jewish organisations and is a national hero in Poland where in 2003 she was awarded its highest distinction, the Order of the White Eagle.

"Irena wasn't even five feet tall, but she walked into the Warsaw Ghetto daily and faced certain death if she was caught," recounted Megan Felt, one of the play's authors. Shortly after Felt and her classmates learned that the woman who had inspired them was still alive, they travelled to Warsaw to meet her thanks to sponsorship from a local Jewish organisation. They found her confined to a wheelchair, the brutal torture by the Gestapo having taken its toll. After each performance of the play, cast members passed around a jar, raising enough money to move Irena into a Catholic nursing home with round-the-clock care. They and their teacher started the Life in a Jar Foundation, which has raised tens of thousands of dollars to help pay for medical and other needs of Holocaust rescuers.

Sir Richard Dannatt, meanwhile, told the BBC of a tattered old Bible he carried around with him on his military campaigns. Yes, it concerned him that some soldiers never came back, but his Bible meditations reminded him that we're all going to die one day, and that the destiny of our souls is of the ultimate importance. As Jesus said, "Greater love has no-one than this that he lay down his life for his friends." And this, of course, is what Christ himself did for mankind.

Persian pressure mounts

News of Iran upgrading its nuclear programme with increased uranium enrichment should ring alarm bells across the nations. They say it is for peaceful purposes but, with a president who has repeatedly declared his wish to see Israel destroyed, it poses a serious worry for the entire Middle East – and the whole world besides. Experts generally agree that the latest advance in Iranian nuclear technology indicates a potential capability for producing a bomb. And with the country having already tested missiles capable of reaching Israel, it is no wonder that the Jewish nation is living in fear. Will the Western nations stand idly by, as they did when Hitler rebuilt the German arsenal, until it is too late?

All the while Iran's growing Christian community is undergoing severe persecution – in some ways comparable to what the Jews suffered under the Nazis in the years leading up to World War II. Some are imprisoned for their faith amidst mounting repression against all who would oppose the state – as many are doing these days – and most of them are converts from Islam who face the criminal charge of apostasy, which could lead to a death sentence. "Every Iranian Muslim knows that to become a Christian involves breaking the law and risking your life," writes ASSIST News Service special correspondent Elizabeth Kendal. "Yet in the midst of this, God is at work and the church is growing. Iranian Christians need our prayers."

But the political struggles in Iran have nothing to do with religious freedom and everything to do with money and lifestyle, according to Ms Kendal. The regime is more than a Shi'ite Muslim theocracy; it is a totalitarian police state whose rulers are protected by an army of Revolutionary Guards along with several million state-sanctioned vigilantes. The opposition – as conservative and Islamist as the ruling regime – objects to President Ahmadinejad's overt belligerence because of its negative economic impact. While subsidies may pacify the impoverished masses, the more pragmatic urban elite want change. What the Iranian Church wants, however, is religious liberty – something that is anathema to Islam.

And yet many Muslims in Iran and other parts of the Middle East are coming to faith in Jesus, often in extraordinary ways through such experiences as visions of Christ! Yes, people deeply embedded in Islamic traditions have been visited from on high – rather as Mary and Joseph were visited by angels in advance of the birth of Christ. So it is no wonder they are prepared to risk their lives for the truth now revealed to them.

We don't wish Iran to be destroyed – which is a possibility if Israel, at least partially supported by America, is attacked or further threatened. Pray for President Ahmadinejad, who apparently has Jewish heritage himself, to realise he is attacking his own people and that his brand of Islam does not advance peace in the Middle East.

CHAPTER 10

Lies, misinformation and Palestinian propaganda

One can only hope for a new era of trust and integrity – especially in the face of so much in the way of lies and misinformation surrounding both the Jewish nation itself, and its people in general.

A Canadian journalist claimed that the facts didn't support the accepted story that a United Nations school was hit by Israeli shells during the Gaza conflict. Writing for the *Canadian Globe and Mail*, Patrick Martin investigated the shelling that led to the tragic deaths of 43 civilians.

He reported: "Physical evidence and interviews with several eye-witnesses, including a teacher who was in the schoolyard at the time of the shelling, make it clear: While a few people were injured from shrapnel landing inside the white-and-blue-walled UN Relief and Works Agency (UNRWA) compound, no-one in the compound was killed. The 43 people who died in the incident were all outside, on the street, where all three mortar shells landed. Stories of one or more shells landing inside the schoolyard were inaccurate."

He added: "While the killing of 43 civilians on the street may itself be grounds for investigation, it falls short of the act of shooting into a schoolyard crowded with refuge-seekers."

Martin's story confirms the under-reported accounts that the Israeli Defence Force accurately returned fire to the location from which it was being shelled by Hamas terrorists who were engaging in what Benjamin Netanyahu referred to as a double war crime – attacking Israeli civilians and hiding behind Palestinian civilians.

There were also claims that Hamas took control of UNRWA food supplies and refused to distribute them to people affiliated with their Fatah rivals. And there were further claims that Hamas took over humanitarian aid and sold it while Palestinians who opposed Hamas's use of their land and homes as launch pads were shot in the legs.

With Palestinians having effectively written off ancient Jewish claims to the Holy Land as fairy tales, meanwhile, it is not surprising there is so much confusion in the current debate over Israel. In something of a political panto-mime, U.S. Vice-President Joe Biden reacted furiously in early 2010 to the fact that his efforts to kick-start a new round of peace negotiations coincided with the approval of plans for building work in the Jewish sector of East Jerusalem, apparently in contravention of international law and definitely in defiance of America's insistence on no further expansion of Jewish homes in disputed territories. Mr Biden said the development risked breaking up the proposed Palestinian state with a series of Jewish enclaves.

The Israelis, however, would be forgiven for seeing it from the opposite perspective in that repeated attempts to divide their land – and their capital – in a bid to placate worldwide demands for a Palestinian state goes against the word of God himself, who thousands of years ago promised the land as their inheritance. And this biblical principle was acknowledged both by the British (in 1917) and the international community who originally granted a homeland for the Jews much greater than the land they presently occupy. Furthermore, division of their land is forbidden in Holy Scripture along with the warning of judgment against nations having a hand in it. And the prophets of old made much of the fact that, after the re-gathering to their ancient homeland of the Jewish people from the north, south, east and west, the ruined cities would be rebuilt.

Ironically, this political dispute coincided with the awarding of medals by the British Government to heroes of the holocaust including 100-year-old Sir Nicholas Winton who rescued hundreds of Jewish children from Prague just before the outbreak of World War II and 91-year-old Denis Avey who helped an Auschwitz inmate survive by swapping places with him – and sharing his supplies – while he was a prisoner-of-war. This 'Holocaust Heroes' ceremony reminded us that there are still many so-called Holocaust deniers, who bury their heads in the sand pretending it never happened so they can feel easier about persecuting Jews today.

In the same way Muslim propaganda now denies ancient Jewish history in order to give credence to their claims to the land. It is a widely held view in the Islamic world that no Jews or tribes of Israel ever lived in the Holy Land. Such views negate the validity of the Bible, with the scriptures being reduced to fairy tales. They hold that neither King David nor King Solomon ever existed, and no temple was built in Jerusalem. PLO founder Yasser Arafat declared that Jesus was 'the first Palestinian' and was nothing to do with Jews or being a descendant of David.

And in an effort to wipe out all evidence of ancient Jewish civilization from the famous Temple Mount area of Jerusalem, the Muslim keepers of the Dome of the Rock mosque have removed hundreds of tons of archeologically rich earth. As for Islam's claim of Jerusalem being their third holiest site, the city is not once mentioned in the Koran and had no special role in the religion until the 1930s.

Sceptical of the true authorship of early Hebrew writings, meanwhile, some modern biblical scholars were convinced that written Hebrew only developed in the sixth century BC. But the discovery of a pottery fragment in an archeological dig in the Valley of Elah – the very place where David fought Goliath – has changed all that. It is dated 3,000 years old, and the Hebrew writing gives further proof of the early settlement of the Jewish people in the Holy Land.

More unhelpful propaganda surrounded the boarding in 2010 of an aid flotilla trying to break Israel's blockade on Gaza (introduced for security reasons), which sparked off predictable fury from the world at large when it led to the killing of nine crew members. As in so many previous cases, the incident was widely portrayed in the media as the bullying Israeli Defence Force overpowering innocent victims who only wished to help ferry much-needed cargo to the stricken Gaza Strip. But the reality was that the crew were at best naïve and more likely exercising a politically-correct belligerent attitude towards a nation who is even seeing her friends desert them. There is no question but that the Israelis came under fierce attack when they boarded the ship. Israel is not against such aid getting to Gaza – they are simply trying to ensure that it doesn't include arms destined to be used against them and it seems perfectly reasonable, therefore, that such ships should dock at Israeli ports.

As Malcolm Hedding of the International Christian Embassy in Jerusalem said: "Any fair-minded person, after viewing the IDF's video footage of the incident, will concede that Israeli commandos were definitely not boarding a shipful of peaceful activists… for embedded among the passengers were a large number of well-armed militants." And in fact it has emerged that these 'activists' were radical Islamic jihadists fully prepared to sacrifice their lives, having left statements to this effect with families and friends. But the international community rushes to condemn Israel before the real facts have emerged.

After all, the blockade of Gaza is because the area is being used as a launching pad for Hamas rockets constantly fired into Israel, who voluntarily gave up this land on which their own people had settled in order to further the cause of peace. But the rockets keep coming. Why? Because the openly stated aim of Hamas is to destroy the Jewish state. Which begs the question as to why it is so unreasonable for Israel to seek to prevent ill-advised friends of Gaza to add fuel to the fire – even if unwittingly acting as couriers of arms? The world's media has already come to its own conclusions, branding Israel as rogues, criminals and pirates. But as a Christian Friends of Israel spokesman said, "Blind arrogance and hatred once again triumphed over reason and truth."

As the ICEJ has stated, the interception was eminently legal, given that several such ships have been used in recent years to ferry arms to Hamas and Hezbollah.

The emergence on the international scene of the Conservative-Liberal Coalition Government in the UK, however, does offer a glimmer of hope on the matter of helping to balance the perception of truth regarding Israel. Part-Jewish himself, Prime Minister David Cameron has stated that "Israel has a right to defend herself", understands the severity of Iran's nuclear threat and has likened Islamic extremism to Nazism. On the other hand, he is part of a consensus of Western political opinion in supporting a 'two-state solution' between Israel and the Palestinians which requires dividing the land and carving up pieces of Jerusalem, something which is proscribed in the Scriptures as an act that would incur the wrath of God. He has also described East Jerusalem as 'occupied territory' and been sharply critical of 'Israeli settlements'. But will he remain a friend of Israel as the rest of the world, including the White House, turns against her?

The Jews – God's chosen people

As the BBC hosted a discussion on the growing anti-Semitism in Britain, it was interesting that even in the studio there was strong antipathy towards Israel. This became clear when everyone clapped at the mention of "what Israel is doing in Gaza", and yet no-one talks of what Gaza is doing to Israel.

The former was a reference to charges of 'war crimes' against Israel for apparently targeting civilians while also responding 'disproportionately' to constant attacks from Gaza simply because Israelis lost fewer soldiers than their counterparts in the conflict. But it is never mentioned that the Israeli Defence Force did something virtually unknown in warfare by dropping leaflets to residents warning of the impending attack to give them time to escape.

Meanwhile cemeteries were desecrated as attacks against Britain's Jewish community more than doubled in a year, with victims even accosted in the streets and a scout group in Essex said to have shouted 'Kill the Jews' to Jewish veterans at the time of the Remembrance Day parades.

The BBC were hosting this debate – on their *Big Questions* Sunday morning TV programme – only days before the Channel 4 *Dispatches* documentary accused them of being biased in favour of Israel. In fact many pro-Israel groups would take the view that the opposite was the case, but it may well have been true that the Beeb had mended their ways somewhat since being told off by the media watchdog for their bias against the Jewish state.

What was clear from the television debate was that no-one, including Jews themselves, seemed to know why they were being persecuted since presenter Nicky Campbell kept asking the question to no avail. I can answer that, perhaps too succinctly and simplistically for some, by stating that it is because they are God's chosen people – both a biblical fact as well as an observational one, with Jews having contributed so much to the world far out of proportion to their numbers.

Christians are also persecuted because they follow Jesus, the Jew, whom they believe to be a fulfilment of the Old Testament law and prophets. Tragically the Jewish perception of Christians was seriously compromised during the Nazi era when some of those sending them to the gas chambers called themselves Christians. And one participant in the BBC programme said the war-time British Government had placed rescued Jewish children with evangelical Christians who would 'force' them to convert.

I couldn't imagine Churchill's government acting in this way, but I do understand how this conclusion has been reached. The fact is evangelical Christians would probably have led the way in offering to adopt Jewish children out of sheer compassion borne out of their faith along with a concern to obey the biblical command to care for God's chosen people. And yes, all who have found Jesus as their Saviour would also want to encourage their Jewish brothers to see him as their true Messiah, but would never 'force' them to accept him.

Meanwhile the Channel 4 *Dispatches* slot concluded that the BBC had capitulated to the Israeli lobby. It sounded like a joke, but they were apparently serious. Though admitting that they had found no conspiracy, they were clearly unhappy with the influence of lobbies such as the Conservative Friends of Israel (and its Labour equivalent) in deciding foreign policy. And then Conservative leader (now Prime Minister) David Cameron was quoted as saying that Israel would be a friend upon whom he would never turn his back as Prime Minister. One simply hopes he lives up to this promise, but some of his statements can be confusing, such as that of his being a Christian who only says his prayers when he goes to church (as he told *Songs of Praise*)!

Standing with Israel is of paramount importance as their very existence is threatened on all sides. Iran keeps threatening to carry out its intention of "wiping Israel off the map" and, with a nuclear capability fast developing, this is far from unrealistic, while Syrian President Bashar Assad talks of the resistance that might be used to 'return' the Golan Heights, no doubt alluding to movements such as Hezbollah. But the Golan Heights are the biblical Bashan, of which God said to Moses that he had "handed over the land…into your hand." Syria now poses an even greater threat as an attack on its southern neighbour might be seen as a useful diversion for the currently beleaguered

Assad.

It is hard to see how the much-pushed two-state solution of dividing ancient Israel – 'giving up territory for peace'– will succeed as every previous attempt in this direction has only sparked more terrorism against the tiny state. The prophet Joel said God would judge those who scattered his people among the nations and divided up their land.

Yes, the Israelis are getting weary of finding solace with the Zionist dream, and it's understandable that they do not see Jesus in a good light because of the history of the so-called Church. Kristallnacht – when Jewish businesses were attacked in Germany – occurred on the birthday of the great Protestant reformer Martin Luther. Yet the New Covenant spoken of by the Jewish prophet Jeremiah related to the Houses of Israel and Judah. "I will put my law in their minds and write it on their hearts. I will be their God, and they will be my people." And the prophet Zechariah spoke of a time when Israel would "look on me, the one they have pierced, and they will mourn for him as one mourns for an only child…"

Gentiles who have already found Christ as Saviour know about his beauty and majesty, but a time is coming when those still looking for their Messiah would at last realise that he has been there all the time. For the prophet Ezekiel foretold that, after they were restored to their own land from all the countries of the earth, he would remove their heart of stone and give them a heart of flesh. And they would live in the land of their forefathers. Jesus is a fulfilment of the Jewish scriptures and, if we love Jesus, we should love the Jews!

CHAPTER 11

Messianic Jews

When Israeli evangelist Tsachi Dahan addressed a Nottinghamshire congregation at a meeting sponsored by the Church's Ministry among Jewish people, co-ordinator Jane Moxon commented that the last time such an envoy had come out of Israel for this purpose was probably in the days of the early church.

That might be debatable, but her point emphasised the extraordinary spiritual phenomenon taking place before our eyes with the resurgence of Jewish belief in Jesus as their Messiah. What was just as special was that Tsachi was speaking fluently in his second language – his native tongue being Hebrew, an ancient language that has recently been revived along with the state of Israel itself and, now too, with the growing numbers of so-called 'Messianic' believers.

Of course, it is worth noting that in the early church it was unusual to be a Gentile, and now it's the other way round, though not for too much longer, if Tsachi has anything to do with it. His dedication to encouraging supporters to spread the gospel among his people is such that he was in England on honeymoon with new wife Angie, fitting in various meetings to promote his work with tourist visits to York, Chatsworth and other jewels of our green and pleasant land.

Tsachi is director of the Dugit Outreach Centre, a bookshop and cafe-based mission in Tel Aviv where, apart from serving good coffee, they are forced to engage in regular spiritual battles with ultra-orthodox religious Jews determined to halt the progress in Israel of the Messianic movement now accounting for up to 25,000 followers – still a small fraction of the country's seven million population.

They turn up to harass and heckle in a bid to dissuade others from joining them, genuinely believing they are doing God a favour by persecuting these

'Jesus preachers'. Jesus had many similar encounters with legalistic religious leaders in his time, and it was in fact the scribes and Pharisees who insisted on his crucifixion. Soon afterwards Saul of Tarsus was so zealous to protect his traditional Jewish faith that he began arresting the early Christians until, on the road to Damascus, he had an amazing encounter with the risen Christ who declared that, in persecuting his followers, he was doing the same to him.

And that is Tsachi's hope for those intimidating the believers who hang out in his Tel Aviv cafe. He recalled a tremendous spiritual victory that occurred after God spoke to his group through a verse from Isaiah (chapter 66, verse 5) during a prayer meeting: "Hear the word of the Lord, 'Your brothers who hate you…have said "Let the Lord be glorified, that we may see your joy!" Yet they will be put to shame…' "

He was immediately filled with such joy that he no longer saw his opponents as a threat. On their next visit, he was so full of the Spirit that he felt able to bless them and tell them how much Yeshua (Jesus) loved them, though he admitted it was still a hard thing to do from a natural, human point of view. And the word was fulfilled following a subsequent confrontation when the fake happiness of his adversary disappeared while the heaviness he had was lifted. "God did something in that place. Something changed in the atmosphere."

The account illustrated the age-old battle being fought between the flesh (human or even humanistic endeavours) and the spirit (when we submit ourselves to God). Abraham, weary of waiting for God's promise of a son through the aged Sarah, tried to force the issue through her maidservant Hagar, with the result that her son Ishmael became an enemy of Isaac, the true heir.

Throughout the ages, said Tsachi, there has been this constant tendency to insist on adding things we have invented ourselves to our religious life, even if in the form of good works, so that we can feel we have qualified for acceptance with our Maker whereas the teaching of the Bible is that God is enough – that there is nothing we can do to earn our salvation. "God is enough for me; his grace is sufficient for me," he said. "We don't need to do anything; there's just a presence to carry."

Tsachi is a former professional dancer who came out of a homosexual lifestyle to embrace the faith he now espouses. "I was always curious about God and what he looks like. My impression as a child was of a gracious and loving grandfather who used to come in his car to sell ice-cream. Then at 23, I started seeking God for answers and he began to reveal his word and truth into my heart. I didn't understand how Jesus connected with a Jewish identity, but I had an encounter with the Lord who really showed himself to me by the way that he loved me on the cross. I was immediately and radically changed."

Yet he wondered if he could still be Jewish if he believed in Yeshua. "Then

I realised God had set me completely free – a Jew who knows his Jewish Messiah and that's it." Referring to the spirit/flesh confrontation, he said: "We see that tension in our country every day. But Jesus is the promise God had for us for thousands of years. A lot of people I speak to never realised Jesus was Jewish. But I tell them that the Old and New Testaments are one."

In the light of the current build-up of increasing hostility towards Israel as the Middle East political crisis deepens, Tsachi says: "There has never been such an urgency for the Jewish people to know Jesus like now." Looking at the map of Israel envisioned by the promoters of the two-state solution, he sees it as a clear fulfilment of Zechariah's prophecy about nations surrounding Jerusalem, whom God will destroy. Israel, he believed, would probably submit itself to compromise "so that God can show himself to them". But they needed to learn to take God's counsel, not that of man.

Orthodox Jew gets 'zapped'

Zipporah Bennett, who was born in New York and raised an orthodox Jew, has been living in Israel since 1976 when she was among the earliest Messianic believers there. She was certainly a pioneer of the Hebraic form of worship adopted by these groups who have grown from just 13 when she first immigrated to around 100. Zipporah was indoctrinated against Jesus and taught never to go near a church because she would be defiled.

"Our people had always been persecuted by these Christians. I learned Hebrew as a child, went to synagogue and celebrated all the feasts. It was a very rich traditional background; this was our identity. But I remember sitting in the synagogue for hours and hours, and looking up and saying to myself: 'I wonder where God is? I should be able to walk and talk with God like Abraham.' And this was the beginning of my spiritual search for ultimate truth. I subsequently went through a whole host of experiences and ended up on the Hawaiian Islands where I couldn't have been further away from Israel. But I was caught up in a (Christian) revival (a restoration of early church enthusiasm and power). I was mean to them. But there was some kind of quality of life to them I didn't have, and I finally succumbed to praying a prayer with them with the idea that I would see what happened. Then they asked: 'Do you want to receive the Holy Spirit?'

"It turned out they were 'charismaniacs' (a teasing reference to so-called Charismatics, who believe the gifts of the Holy Spirit are as valid today as they were in the early church). Well, I didn't have any problem with that because I knew from our Scriptures that it said, right at the beginning, 'The Spirit of God was hovering over the face of the deep.' That's Jewish enough for me, I thought, and as they laid hands on me a wave of heat went over me from head to toe. I got zapped. But a tremendous battle went on inside me afterwards. My mind couldn't fathom what had happened in my spirit. But my friends began to show me how the Old Testament pointed to Jesus, and it was a powerful awakening to see this portrait of the Jewish Messiah who has been dressed up in Gentile clothing."

Her heart was changed, as prophesied in Ezekiel 36, and she subsequently helped to fulfil many other biblical prophecies which foretell the return of Jews from all corners of the earth in the last days – Hawaii being about as far as you can get from Israel. "I believe God was telling me to go, and I emigrated in 1976." She said there were only some 300 Messianic believers in Israel at the time, but that the numbers have since increased some fifty-fold with groups meeting in every city, 800 attending a recent youth conference and the existence of 24-hour 'houses of prayer and worship'. "God is doing a work in our land, but you've got to fight tooth and nail to get anyone into the kingdom there," she admitted. She believed we were experiencing a transitional period in which the 'days of the Gentiles' (in Israel) was giving way to full Jewish restoration. Current world troubles such as the Middle East uprisings, street riots, extraordinary weather patterns and financial collapse were the 'birth-pangs' announcing the imminent return of the Messiah, she explained. The time wasn't far away when "the people walking in darkness (specifically in Israel) will again see a great light, as they did once before when Jesus trod the hills of Galilee at his first coming. All Israel would soon look upon the One they had pierced and mourn for him as for an only son, in fulfilment of Zechariah's prophecy.

The Way, the Truth and the Life

The reality of the Messianic fellowships came home to me when Yossi Ovadia, one of their pastors, came to speak to our Prayer for Israel gathering in the South Yorkshire town of Doncaster run by Alan and Daphne Brooke, who lived in Israel for some years. Yossi leads a congregation of 120 in the Galilee area. With a Hebrew name meaning The Way, it was founded in 1989, has multiplied tenfold in 20 years and has already given birth to a daughter fellowship in the Valley of Jezreel – the projected venue for Armageddon no less. The fellowship, in the town of Karmiel, is surrounded by Arab villages (Arabs outnumber Jews in this northern part of Israel) but these believers are passionate about building good relationships with their Arab neighbours. And indeed Jews and Arabs worship Jesus (Yeshua) together in their meetings. Not only that, but they have a regular conference dedicated to the ideal of reconciliation with their brothers in Christ, which is in stark contrast to how things are portrayed in the mainstream media.

Another extraordinary venture in which this fellowship is engaged is the Hand to Hand (Yad b Yad) movement, through which teenage Jewish believers are hosted by families in Germany where, after a week of fellowship, they visit the notorious Auschwitz death camp together, comforting one another as they pray in the gas chambers facing up to the horrors of its history but fortified by their faith in the One who sacrificed his life for us all on the cross and after-wards sharing communion in memory of this wonderful act by their shared Messiah "and to look to the future with hope because of what Christ has done for them, and that with Jesus they can overcome".

I was also moved by the lengths these Messianic fellowships have to go in order to share their faith with other Israelis. Many in their congregation are new immigrants from Russia, others speak only Hebrew and then there are those from an English-speaking background. There are, in fact, 15 different nations represented including Portuguese and Romanian Jews. So preaching, and singing, has constantly to be translated. It's a bit like a United Nations of believers. And that is how Yossi and others want it. There are churches specifically for Russians, but he doesn't believe in such ethnically-based groups – rather that the nation is represented by all its many parts proving their oneness in the Messiah who unites them all. It was a sacrifice for the Russians, he explained, because the language problem proved such a barrier. But the fruit of unity was worth it.

It was clear that the major Jewish feasts like Purim, Succoth and Passover are celebrated in great style by Yossi's flock, though baptism in the Jordan is also practiced. They are no less Jewish for embracing the Christ of Christians because, in fact, it is we Christians who have embraced the Jewish Messiah – largely rejected by his people when he came 2,000 years ago, it is true, but increasingly accepted in these last days in fulfilment of ancient prophecy. And in any case, these feasts are a stark reminder of what God has done in deliver-ing his chosen people from bondage and annihilation.

He pointed out that from the dozen fellowships that existed at the time our hosts were in Israel in the early 1980s, there were now more than 100. And though they still represented less than half a per cent of the population, it was a significant increase – a trickle that could soon turn into a flood.

Yossi clearly saw the restoration of Israel in the two stages we have already outlined – a re-gathering of Jews to the land that would once again become fruitful with its long desolated cities being rebuilt followed by a change of heart in the nation when they would at last recognise Jesus as their Messiah.

Yossi is associated with Messianic Testimony, a mission supporting such congregations. And for those who think there are different roads to God, he has this to say: "There is only one way to God for both Jews and Gentiles, and that's through Jesus."

Rabbi embraces Jesus

And then there was Rabbi Harold Vallins, a British-born Jew who, after spending many of his teenage years as a "confirmed fanatical atheist", became a rabbi as a 29-year-old in 1970 after being shown by another rabbi how wonderful Judaism could be. And in 1981 he moved to Melbourne, Australia, to lead a congregation. There he formed a strong friendship with a neighbouring Christian minister and, in 1997, began attending a breakfast prayer meeting with him. After a few weeks, Harold was asked to close the meeting with a prayer and found himself concluding it with the words, 'Through Jesus Christ our Lord, Amen.' Harold recalled: "It took me a week to recover from that. I didn't dare tell anyone what I had done. I had been brought up never to mention the name of Jesus and now I had prayed to him. I decided the best thing to do was to keep quiet about the whole thing and not say a word to anyone."

A little later, however, at a worship conference with the prayer group, something amazing occurred. Harold said: "As prayer was being recited I felt as though I was being transformed onto another plane of life. I suddenly knew that Jesus was in the room with us. I could actually feel Jesus come and stand behind me and put his hand upon my shoulder. And I could hear myself saying, inside my head, 'Jesus, you are my Messiah, my Lord, my Saviour'."

On the final night Harold found himself on the stage and told the audience that he was a rabbi and that he had just accepted Jesus as his Saviour and Messiah. But there was a great cost involved, for he was forced to resign his position, lost many of his dear friends and his wife divorced him. And yet his new-found joy outweighed the pain for Harold. He said: "I'm a Jew and will always remain a Jew. I've become a Jewish follower of a Jewish Messiah. I'm a fulfilled Jew, a completed Jew. A Jew can hope and pray to be forgiven of sins, but is never certain of this. It is only through Jesus' death that we can be sure of God's forgiveness."

Harold died in June 2009.

In a similar vein, I love the story told in his daily devotional meditations* by the legendary Welsh revivalist Selwyn Hughes of the prayer offered at an informal White House prayer group by a Jewish man named Arthur Burns. A man of some distinction who was chairman of the United States Federal Reserve System at the time, he was not a Christian but seemed to enjoy being present at the prayer meetings. Naturally the Christians there treated him with respect even though they found it difficult to involve him in the proceedings. For example, different people would be asked to close in prayer, but Arthur would always be passed by. One day, however, the group was led by a newcomer who did not know the situation. At the end of the session he turned to Arthur Burns and asked him to close in prayer. Hesitating for a moment, he then prayed this prayer: "Lord, I pray that you would bring Jews to know Jesus Christ. I pray that you would bring Muslims to know Jesus Christ. Finally, Lord, I pray that you would bring Christians to know Jesus Christ. Amen."

Selwyn added: "His refreshing directness quite startled those present, but they took the point: those who already know Jesus need to know him better if they are to reflect his amazing grace to the world around. Rarely are Christians indicted for being too much like Jesus; far more commonly they are charged with not being sufficiently Christlike.

Disabled couple join battle for Israel

During a protracted journalists' strike (which I didn't join) I took the opportunity afforded by the need to produce extra copy to interview a Yorkshire couple who had recently been appointed regional representatives for an influential organisation set up to support Israel.

Roy and Christine Sherrard, who are members of a church in Selby, near York, believe Christians owe everything to the Jews and are now looking after a large section of Yorkshire for Christian Friends of Israel. And though both are disabled with an acute form of fibro-myalgia (causing widespread pain and chronic fatigue), they are slowly finding their feet in the demanding new role to which they believe God has called them.

"It's a struggle for both of us," says Christine. "For example, we go to a twice-yearly conference in Gateshead (north-east England), after which it took us a week to recover on one occasion with me aching and feeling so ill. We made all the excuses why we couldn't take on this role. Then we heard some teaching about Moses and all the excuses he gave God as to why he wasn't up to the task of leading the Israelites out of Egypt."

One of Moses' complaints was that he wasn't up to public speaking, and among the symptoms of the condition particularly affecting Christine is that she sometimes completely loses the thread of what she is saying. "So we decided to pray about it and eventually accepted. So here we are – two cripples willing to work for God."

Roy is a former coal miner who moved to Selby from Leeds to work at the Riccall Mine and Christine is a qualified adult tutor with a degree in social science. They actually met through a support group for their condition and were married seven years ago. And when Christine, who was brought up in the Salvation Army, was asked to lead prayer at the group on the occasion of the first anniversary of 9/11 – because they knew she was a Christian – Roy was so struck by the reality of what he heard that he too was drawn to the faith. "It was the first time I'd heard a prayer in twenty years. I'd moved away from church and I wanted to know more."

So she invited him to a businessmen's evangelistic meeting near Selby where he committed his life to Christ. What puzzled him, however, was why the speaker had also brought a big Israeli flag with him – 'What had this to do with Christianity,' he asked?

"As a result of that we got to know more about the roots of our faith and wanted to start something similar in Selby. We discovered that Jesus, by his death on the cross, was our Passover Lamb – a fulfilment of what the enslaved Jews were commanded to do on the eve of their escape from Egypt which was to daub their doorposts with the blood of a sacrificial lamb at the sight of which the Angel of Death would 'pass over' them, sparing the first-born of their households from the judgment meted out against Pharaoh for refusing to let God's people go. Those meetings proved the catalyst for taking us back to our Hebraic roots which in turn led us to a deeper relationship with Jesus.

"After all, virtually the entire Bible (Old and New Testament) was written by Jews, Jesus was Jewish, his disciples were Jewish… It's a Jewish faith! Jesus is the one all the prophets of old spoke about. It's been an unfolding revelation: the more we've studied and got back to our roots, the greater has become our love for the Jewish people who have been persecuted to the hilt through the centuries. But they have kept the Word of God – a precious gift – for us and we owe them a debt of gratitude. We just want to bless the Jewish people. It's like when you first meet the love of your life – you want to give them things."

One example was a badly injured Israeli soldier they heard about on the news. "I felt like he was my own son and became greatly burdened for him," Christine told me. "So I wanted to send him gifts, but had no idea where he was. So I got onto an Israeli-based internet site selling items such as prayer shawls and it so happened that the man in charge was just 20 minutes away from the hospital where this particular soldier was being treated and was able to deliver our gifts. He has since recovered."

Roy and Christine are not Jews – preferring to call themselves Messianic Gentiles in identifying with the increasing number of Jews around the world acknowledging Jesus as their Messiah. And it's the worship in Jewish settings that Roy finds so powerful. "It even involves dancing, which is not in itself a pleasure to me – I have the proverbial two left feet – but this is a new dimension."

Christine added: "As Christians we believe we are called to bless Israel, the only nation with which God has made a covenant. He made it with Abraham, Isaac and Jacob and their descendants for all time and has never changed his mind. And God has demonstrated his faithfulness to this covenant by preserving the Jews as an identifiable people and restoring them to their land in fulfilment of the scriptures. The Jewish people have been shamefully mistreated throughout history, often by people who call themselves Christians. But God has said that he would bless those who blessed them, and curse those who cursed them. And although we don't always agree with what Israel does, as her friends we will always stand by her and with her."

Jewish man with a Jesus message

Also based in Selby is a former Orthodox Jew now working to persuade his people that Jesus is, after all, their Messiah. Adrian Glasspole is the national evangelist for the Church's Ministry among Jewish people (CMJ) – an organisation set up over 200 years ago by the likes of William Wilberforce which, as we have already outlined, has played a significant part in the restoration to the Promised Land of millions of Jews in recent years.

With one family member shot in the woods near Minsk in Belarus as part of a massacre by Nazis in 1942 at the time millions of his kindred were being herded into death camps, Adrian is all too aware of the difficulties of presenting Christ as the Saviour of his people in view of the shocking persecution so often meted out in his name. As he points out, Hitler died a Catholic but has still not been excommunicated – not even for the murder of six million people!

So how did an Orthodox Jew become a follower of Jesus? With a slave ship captain ancestor who married a slave girl, and another at one-time Governor-General of Jamaica, Adrian was born in Glastonbury, Somerset – "the New Age capital of the world". And because he felt forced into the merchant navy at 16, he lost contact with his teenage love Dawn. But 30 years later she got in touch with him through Facebook, and they got married in 2009.

Once at sea he realised he could die – he almost did on his first ship – and became interested in religion as a result. And because he was Jewish, he got in touch with the Rabbi on his return to Bristol. In due course he became a convinced follower of an Orthodox sect that believed the Messiah *had* come in the form of a certain Rabbi called Schneerson (who died in 1994), who was not only a genius with nine degrees and a fluent multi-linguist, but also a miracle worker.

Then he started meeting Christians who talked about Jesus. "The crunch time came and I realised the Messiah had come, and that he was either the

'Rebbe' – a term of endearment for the leader of the fiercely anti-missionary sect I had been following – or Jesus of Nazareth. So I sat with a cup of coffee and a cigarette in my digs one Saturday night, praying: 'God, show me who this Jesus of Nazareth really is,' and he did! It was not a vision, but I saw a Jewish man hanging on a cross and that changed the course of my history. I was 31 and about to graduate from university."

After a time of hotel management which included the Bristol Hilton and running his own restaurant, he found he couldn't stop telling people about Jesus and subsequently completed a theology course after which he set up the UK branch of a New York-based outreach to Jews in Manchester. In due course he was 'head-hunted' by CMJ.

Explaining his calling, he said: "If Jesus is the Messiah, then Jewish people need to know. And even if he isn't, and he's just one of the greatest teachers who ever lived, then people need to know what it was he taught that was so great." And he admits that, though Jews are won over, people like himself are seen at best as apostates or deluded – he has even been called a 'spiritual Nazi'. "But I can understand why that is in view of the history of the church which has persecuted Jews over the centuries."

Adrian believes there is just one word that sums up his mission – and that is reconciliation, whether between Jews and Arabs, or Jews and Gentiles.

Actually, Jews have been reaching out to their own people for some time – in the modern era I mean, as of course the twelve apostles were all Jewish and did not really understand that the gospel was meant for any other people at all until St Peter finally grasped the fact as a result of a supernatural vision in Joppa which coincided with the visit of men from the household of a devout Roman centurion (Cornelius) who himself had received an angelic visitation directing his servants there.

Eddie Levine, grandfather of Rachelle Hocking, a friend of mine, was a pioneer missionary among the many Jews of South Africa. An Egyptian Jew, he was thrown out of the family home upon his understanding that Jesus was their Messiah. He married Eunice Pillemer, a South African, and they worked in that country for the Haddesah Jewish Christian Youth Movement before joining the British Jews Society, thus becoming – in 1951 – their first missionaries in South Africa which was to become a fruitful field of work with large Jewish populations in many of its major cities, particularly Johannesburg where, with some suburbs almost exclusively Jewish, it earned the nickname 'Jewburg'.

Among Eddie's notable converts was the Jewish singer Al Preston who himself became an evangelist to his people through his music. The South African branch of the BJS (entitled the South African Society for the Propaga-tion of the Gospel among the Jews) became the largest outside the UK and also supported the mission's outreach in Haifa, Israel, by sending a doctor for the medical work there.

Eddie had something of a comic 'Laurel and Hardy' relationship with his partner and director, Julius Katz, according to the memoirs of another pioneer, Ernest Lloyd. Both spoke with strong accents and the story goes that Eddie was instructed to tap his watch when Julius had overrun his time at the pulpit. But when he dutifully did so on one occasion and Katz appeared not to have noticed, Eddie began gesticulating with exaggerated movements which finally attracted the attention of his boss who stopped in mid-sentence by scolding: "Eddie, vhy are you distractink me? Please sit down and be quiet!"

Rachelle recalls: "Granddad could speak seven languages, including Afrikaans. He was very well known in many Dutch Reformed churches and was often invited to preach (in Afrikaans) and sing. The one my mom remembers most fondly was the DRC in Kensington, Johannesburg. My grandmother Eunice was Al Preston's first cousin (he changed his name from Pillemer, perhaps for showbiz reasons). My great aunt Maisie Pillemer carried on the work of the BJS South African branch after my granddad died in the USA and she served as president of the Hebrew Christian Alliance in South Africa for many years."

It ought to be said at this point, for the record, that a form of 'replacement theology' (already referred to) was played out in South Africa with disastrous consequences though, mercifully, the church there has since repented of this and a great revival movement has resulted. The original Dutch settlers who took part in the Great Trek of 1838 in an attempt to get away from the stifling rule of the British at the Cape saw themselves as Israelites and South Africa as their Promised Land. Their British enemies were their Egyptian persecutors and the black inhabitants the godless Canaanites who were to be subjugated. This skewed worldview of course paved the way for the system of apartheid, through which black South Africans were second-class citizens fit only to be "hewers of wood and drawers of water" for their white masters.

But the Afrikaners, and the Dutch Reformed Church which influenced much of their thinking, are still thankfully people of The Book without which a relatively bloodless transition to black majority rule would not have taken place. South Africa's first black president Nelson Mandela fully understood the history and sincerity of the Afrikaners, and treated them as such with due respect. Now, having dispensed with a slanted interpretation of the Bible which led them astray, the indigenous white people of southern Africa are back on the right path as convinced as ever that the Book's author provides the only true course to follow in life.

Living and working under fire

Many Israelis live in a state of constant fear from the threat of rocket attacks, suicide bombers and invasion – they have already been through a series of wars in their short history which is only a year older than I am – but a British couple I have known for some years now actually chose to volunteer for the 'the front line' in an effort to help the fledgling state. Dentist Alan Brooke (who died in October 2011, aged 82) and his wife Daphne left the comfort of beautiful Cornwall to live and work in Israel from 1979-85. These were still early days in the development of the new state and they heard that there was a desperate need of dentists, especially for children.

They had their "eyes opened" to the issues surrounding Israel through Middle East expert and well-known Jewish prophetic speaker Lance Lambert and in due course felt God was calling them there. So they upped sticks with two teenagers who had not yet left home (their other two children were respectively studying medicine and nursing) and initially spent a year in Jerusalem where Alan worked in an Orthodox Jewish school for boys.

The family attended a Messianic congregation which included Arabs, one of whom was in the leadership team. After that they spent two-and-a-half years in Tiberias (Galilee) where Alan worked in a kibbutz and also helped out in the clinic of a Jewish dentist from England. During this time they moved up close to the Lebanon border where, alongside working in a kibbutz, Alan also went into South Lebanon – on an army pass – as almost every dentist had fled in the ongoing strife. He provided emergency service in very primitive conditions in a hospital run by French-speaking nuns – the chair would collapse while the patient was undergoing treatment and the water would go off without warning!

They came under shelling from rocket fire during the 1982 conflict. "I suppose it was frightening," Daphne admitted, "but we were so certain it was where God wanted us to be we didn't actually feel frightened. We actually spent two nights in a bomb shelter with all the neighbours, and on one of those nights we were entertaining two missionaries from Africa, who joined us in taking cover.

"It was a very special time in our lives," Daphne recalled. "In Jerusalem you just felt you were at the centre of things. Everything had significance and the Bible came alive to us. The people didn't seem to dwell on trivialities; there wasn't this obsession with entertainment along with shallow talking and thinking. Life to them had real significance because of all they had suffered in the past and still do suffer, and so they concentrated on the really important things in life."

Alan and Daphne would have stayed longer in Israel had there been a clear need to continue but, once the door opened for Russian Jews to emigrate there, enough dentists arrived to meet the demand. However, the sacrificial giving of six years of their lives would no doubt have helped to produce untold benefits for the new state of Israel.

FOOTNOTES
*Every Day With Jesus, published by Crusade for World Revival

CHAPTER 12

The real Middle East peace process

We all know there are times in life when we can't see the wood for the trees. So it is in the political world today, especially in the case of the Middle East where few are able to spot the sparkling gem that is the emerging state of Israel for the piles of dust and rubble that surround it.

Though indeed a melting pot of trouble, what is happening there is actually a true miracle of our times both as far as people and politics are concerned. While the media portrays Israelis and Palestinians as sworn enemies and the political problem they represent as pretty much intractable as the peace process stumbles and staggers, there is in fact something remarkable happening beneath the surface and almost invisible to the natural eye that, with further growth and encouragement, will solve all these problems. Arab and Jew are gradually making peace with one another, and an increasing number of politicians are gaining a significant insight into the troubles which could well pave the way for a new era.

For example, there are Arab Christians meeting all over the nation praying for Israel and holding out the hand of fellowship to their Jewish brothers while a growing number of Messianic congregations, some including Jews and Arabs, believe that Jesus – the Prince of Peace – is indeed the Messiah both of Jews and Gentiles. This has led to much reconciliation between previously opposing factions. But there are also distinctive Arab congregations, which include former Muslims, who have the same understanding.

The New Covenant Church in Haifa, for one, is growing fast and reaching out to surrounding Arab nations via an internet radio station. At Mount Carmel, near Haifa, a Messianic congregation has strong relations with local Arab pastors and a significant number of people – both Jews and Arabs – are turning to Yeshua (Jesus). And there is an Arab fellowship in Jerusalem's Old City which has strong links with Messianic (Jewish) pastors. Also in Jerusalem is the Community of Reconciliation, sharing the gospel with people either hostile or indifferent to Jesus. There is a growing understanding both among Jews and Arabs that Jesus is their only hope and there is increasing evidence that Jews and Arabs are living, working and even praying together in Israel. He is indeed the only hope for world peace, especially in the Middle East.

The only problem is that this sort of thinking is both politically incorrect and forbidden territory to both sides of the divide. But with more and more Jews coming to recognise Yeshua as their true Messiah, and Muslims also converting to Yesooa (Jesus in Arabic), both groups are finding true peace through this common bond.

In one part of Israel an Arab pastor, Shmuel Aweida, leads a Jewish 'Messianic' congregation in Haifa and had the unenviable task of having to bury a child victim of a terrorist attack. And a Jewish woman called Lisa Miera has managed through her faith in Christ to overcome the bitterness she felt over a violent attack on her soldier son captured on film. She came face to face with one of the key assailants in court and had the courage to say: "In the name of Yeshua, the Messiah, I forgive you."

The man was given a ten-year jail sentence and Lisa was making arrangements to visit him in prison to talk about peace at the time a documentary film 'Forbidden Peace – the story behind the headlines' was being produced by London-based Jews for Jesus.

Moran Rosenblit and Taysir Abu Saada (otherwise known as Tass) started out on opposing sides and are now brothers in Christ living in exile in the United States. Moran says: "There is a temporary fix in the deals of the politicians. But when Jews and Arabs come together in the name of the true God there is a true peace." He recalls how his heart was filled with hatred after several of his friends were among 22 soldiers who died at the hands of a suicide bomber. He felt as if there was no more value for human life in Israel and left for America.

Meanwhile Tass, a Palestinian, developed hatred towards the Jewish people "because they took my land...so I hated them with a passion and fought with Yasser Arafat's Palestine Liberation Organisation."

He later became a successful restaurateur and it was a customer who introduced him to Jesus. And though a devout Muslim who had travelled to Mecca several times, he said he found peace and joy and "a burden that lifted off my shoulder like a mountain." He said it "blew him away" when he discovered the Bible promised that the descendants of Ishmael as well as Isaac (the children of Abraham) would be blessed by God – the Arab race comes from Ishmael and the Jewish from Isaac.

He met Moran in 2001 and they became close. But Moran was at first reluctant until his new friend asked forgiveness for his friends who had died. "And I asked him to forgive me for my hatred for the Arabs." Yet he admitted: "Even after I accepted the Lord a good Arab for me was a dead Arab."

And Tass felt likewise: "I had a passion for killing a Jew." But he discovered that Jesus prayed for the forgiveness of those who had nailed him to the cross because they didn't know what they were doing. "If he can forgive so much, I can forgive so little." Now he says: "I would give my life for the soul of a Jew." And speaking of Moran, he says: "He's my little brother who means everything to me. And no-one except God can bring that about between two fierce enemies." He added: "It's not just a conflict in the Middle East. It's a conflict in our own lives."

Moran said that those who allowed Messiah Jesus to enter their hearts would be filled with a tremendous love, joy and peace. One convert described Jesus as "the cure for the human soul", adding: "I have to share it with others even if it means my life may be taken." She was referring to the serious threats converts face, especially in the Muslim culture, although Jews who follow Jesus are also made to feel they have betrayed their faith and yet, as Moran said, "it's the most Jewish thing you can do" if indeed he is the Messiah to which the entire Jewish scriptures point.

The film also features Rahel, an Israeli Jew who drives to Palestinian zones to pick up guests for her home where Jews and Arabs sit side by side listening to stories about Jesus. "I can't see any hope except him," she said. Joseph Haddad, an Arab, spoke of how Jesus gave him peace with God and the power to forgive his enemies. He had mistreated his parents and his wife, but was now reconciled with them all. "Only God can do such things in the life of a man," he said. And the film ends with the poignant story of a friendship in old age between a Jewish and Arab woman in Haifa "sharing in daily tasks and eternal promises" as they live out their days in the love of Christ.

Another remarkable story revolves around Mosab Hassan Yousef, the son of a Hamas terrorist leader, who grew up in a culture where hating Israelis went without question. Then, after being tortured in an Israeli prison, he discovered that Hamas was torturing its own people, which forced him to reconsider all he had taken for granted. And when he met Christians, who gave him a Bible, he was astounded to read that Jesus told us to love our enemies, which opened his eyes to the fact that evil, not man, lay behind the problems of the Middle East.

In his book, *Son of Hamas*, he records how he became a double agent for Israeli intelligence, providing information that saved innocent lives, but was eventually unable to keep up the double life and fled to America where he was granted asylum. However, he has paid a high price for his faith and courage as family and friends have turned their backs on him. In an interview with *New Life* (*http://www.newlife.co.uk/*) he says: "I remain very grateful that I didn't turn into a suicide bomber, and instead looked for the root of the problem. When Middle Eastern nations – Jews and Arabs alike – start to understand some of what I understand, only then will there be peace."

Politicians throw light on the subject!

Meanwhile former Prime Minister of Spain Jose Maria Aznar, in a Times article, threw some light on the subject when he urged support for Israel because "if it goes down, we all go down". He and a group of prominent international politicians were forming a new Friends of Israel group. Their political judgment is that 'the red mists of anger' are clouding our judgment about Israel. While not defending any specific policy or the Israeli government, he argues that Israel is at the cutting edge in the battle between militant Islam and the West and concludes: "Israel is a fundamental part of the West which is what it is thanks to its Judeo-Christian roots. If the Jewish element of those roots is upturned and Israel lost, then we are lost too. Whether we like it or not our fate is inextricably intertwined."

And Britain's former Prime Minister Tony Blair, who has been living in Israel as Middle East envoy for the Quartet (Russia, the U.S., the United Nations and the European Union), has been making a lot of sense on the issue of 'de-legitimisation' of which, he says, there are two forms. There are those who openly question Israel's right to exist, but at least we know where we are with them. The other is more insidious and harder to spot, but amounts to a refusal to accept that Israel has a legitimate point of view.

It is harder to deal with, he says, because many of those engaging in it would fiercely deny they are doing so. "It is this form that is in danger of growing, and whose impact is potentially highly threatening, in part because it isn't obvious. I would define it in this way: it is a conscious or often unconscious resistance, sometimes bordering on refusal, to accept Israel has a legitimate point of view – note that I say refusal to accept Israel has a legitimate point of view. I'm not saying refusal to agree with it. People are perfectly entitled to agree or not; but rather an unwillingness to listen to the other side, to acknowledge that Israel has a point, to embrace the notion that this is a complex matter that requires understanding of the other way of looking at it."

And later in the communication from which this excerpt is taken, Mr Blair illustrates his assertion in this way: "A constant conversation I have with some, by no means all, of my European colleagues is to argue to them: don't apply rules to the Government of Israel that you would never dream of applying to your own country. In any of our nations, if there were people firing rockets, committing acts of terrorism and living next door to us, our public opinion would go crazy. And any political leader who took the line that we shouldn't get too excited about it wouldn't last long as a political leader. This is a democracy. Israel lost 1,000 citizens to terrorism in the intifada. That equates in UK population terms to 10,000. I remember the bomb attacks from (Irish) Republican terrorism in the 1970s. There weren't many arguing for a policy of phlegmatic calm."

Among those fitting this prejudicial and irrational category are the Methodists who voted to boycott Israeli goods – a shocking departure from the passionately held views of their founders John and Charles Wesley that the Jews should be restored to their land.

The issue of legitimacy is further clouded by ongoing rhetoric over Israel's so-called occupation and the building of new settlements in such areas. Israel believes Judea, Samaria and the West Bank have been promised them by God and, indeed, under the British Government's Balfour Declaration of 1917, later ratified by the League of Nations (the predecessor to the UN) this land, and much more, was promised as a homeland for the Jewish people. But President Barack Obama has promised to help end "an occupation that began in 1967" when Israeli soldiers re-captured territory illegally taken from them in the War of Independence. And since the hope of successful peace negotiations rests almost entirely on an agreement to create a separate Palestinian state, which would include East Jerusalem as its capital (thereby dividing both the land and its capital), a resolution is far from probable. As I've already said, it goes clean against God's own edict (in the Holy Bible) that the land he promised to Abraham and his descendants was not to be divided, and nations who had a hand in doing so would be judged. And it is hardly a practical solution to allow once-implacable foes who have been harbouring terrorists right on your doorstep an even more convenient platform from which to further de-stabilise the country's security. And in any case Palestinian Authority chairman Mahmoud Abbas has said: "No Jewish Israel citizens will be allowed to set foot inside the new Palestinian state." What sort of friendly gesture is that? And besides, Jerusalem's Old City has a Jewish quarter who have been living there for centuries. What will happen to them?

The whole thing has been further complicated by the increasingly provocative statements of Muslim sympathy from President Obama which somewhat defies his declared Christian credentials at the time of his presidential campaign. But though apparently sure of himself, President Obama is in trouble with his electorate over a number of issues. Selwyn Duke, on the American Thinker website, quotes author G K Chesterton as saying, "There was a time when men weren't very sure of themselves, but they were very sure of what the truth was. Now men are very sure of themselves but not at all sure of what the truth is." In Duke's view, the latter describes Obama. "If he does have faith, it is in himself. And that is a faith terribly misplaced."

But as I keep saying, there is a growing body of Jews around the world who are placing their trust in Yeshua (Jesus), their Messiah, having discovered the 'pearl of great price' – that the One they thought was for Christians only actually came for the Jew first, and then, through them, would also reach the Gentiles through the efforts of apostles like Peter and Paul. I do not apologise for repeating once again (because it's a truth that will take time to recover) that the early Church was almost entirely Jewish; it is estimated that within a generation of Pentecost, some 100,000 people – about half the population of Jerusalem at the time – were followers of the risen Christ. Sadly, the church became too 'Christianised' over the centuries and, exacerbated by misguided persecution, Jews gradually retreated to the synagogue. Now, however, there is a spiritual awakening of God's ancient people, again as the Scriptures foretold through prophecies such as that of Ezekiel about giving them "a new heart and a new spirit, removing the heart of stone and replacing it with a heart of flesh".

There are now over a hundred Messianic fellowships in Israel where Jews and Arab believers share their lives in love and harmony in fulfilment of St Paul's prophecy about "the one new man" bringing about peace through the death of Christ on the cross of Calvary, "destroying the dividing wall of hostility".

Prayer For Israel director Derek Rous, in one of the movement's bulletins, drew our attention to what he calls "the greatest reality of our times" by writing: "The Spirit of God is at work today in the lives of believers in Yeshua who in this generation are a living testimony on the streets, in the homes, at work, in the schools, in the shops, almost anywhere in Israel where there are Jewish people. Bearing witness to the Messiah Jesus is happening largely unnoticed, using natural and considerate approaches to their neighbours in the course of their daily lives, not just in word but also in deed. Surely this is the most exciting development to stir the hearts of true believers in our times. Bringing Jews and Arabs to faith in Jesus and the development of the Messianic Body, made up of Jewish and Arab believers, is surely the greatest concern of our hearts. This 'peace process' – bringing in the 'one new man' – is a true miracle of our times."

Have you spotted the pearl of great price – and purchased it?

A heart-felt bridge to peace

Against a background in which they are portrayed by much of the media as the oppressor, many Jewish people are actually doing everything they can to help their Arab neighbours and live at peace with them. One extraordinary example of this is to be found at the Wolfson Medical Centre in Tel Aviv, where Israeli doctors are fighting to save the lives of Palestinian children with congenital heart defects. And a Christian organisation called Shevet Achim is acting as the go-between, raising funds to bring children from the neighbouring Gaza Strip and other Arab lands lacking adequate medical facilities across the border to Israel. It costs $3,500 (£1,750) to rescue each child, who would otherwise have no hope of survival. This is the price of keeping volunteers in the field and providing the funding to allow the doctors to continue their work.

Heading up the organisation is former journalist Jonathan Miles, who describes the treatment of the babies in Israel as "a very moving experience". After receiving little or no hospital care in Gaza, the baby suddenly becomes an emergency in Israel. "Though most of the Jewish doctors are secular (not God-conscious), where human life is concerned they will stay up all night and even come in on a weekend."

He told of one doctor who was holidaying on his sailing boat. But when he heard of a Palestinian child's condition, he turned his boat around to see what he could do. There is no Arab-Israeli conflict in the hospital. "It is such a beautiful thing to see," said Jonathan. "Every division falls away. A spirit of grace is being released that has eternal significance – seeing these two peoples coming together."

He describes his organisation as "an 'underground railroad' bringing dying children past the barriers of religious division which would keep them from a new life." And after helping four Iraqi children come to Israel for heart surgeries in 2006, dozens were able to come the following year, with each one's story carefully documented on their website – *http://www.shevet.org* – and they keep raising funds to bring more Iraqi and other children to Israel for heart surgery.

Shevet Achim is a Hebrew phrase taken from Psalm 133 which talks of the blessing of brothers living together in unity. In a video of the work, one doctor is heard to say: "These little guys and their families may be a bridge to peace." Those who have been helped are profoundly touched when they realise Christians have reached out to them because Jesus tells them to love their neighbour as themselves. An Iraqi Kurd said: "I think God gave my child a bad heart so I could come here and learn about the true God."

Jonathan said Israelis are very willing to do things for their neighbours – in fact they are willing to do anything for peace. But there is so much ignorance and misinformation – among Christians, Jews and Muslims – about each other. One Russian immigrant who is among a growing number of Jews to have discovered Jesus as Messiah said it all began when she heard that Jesus was a Jew.

However, news of their work has provoked indignation among some Muslim movements, who refuse to believe there is any philanthropic motive behind it. And they suggest the 'Zionists' are stealing the children's organs. But others, like one Arabic reformist website, have carried more positive reader responses like "Thank you Israel for helping the Iraqi kids".

Says Jonathan: "The edifices of hatred, lies and division are being shaken by the simple act of loving and caring for these children. Try as they might to condemn it, the Association of Muslim Scholars in Iraq end up by asking 'Why doesn't anyone else care about us?' Children are also now being brought in from Jordan. And individuals and church groups are encouraged to sponsor a child through the medical process. For more details log onto their website at *http://www.shevet.org*

Muslims dream of Jesus

Meanwhile thousands of Muslim people across the world are having encounters with Jesus Christ through dreams, visions and personal visitations, according to British missionary Paul Tew. Originally based in North Nottinghamshire, Paul works for Open Doors which has been established for more than 50 years under its founder Brother Andrew, a Dutchman who became notorious for smuggling Bibles through the Iron Curtain. The mission was started to help Christians stand firm in their faith in the face of persecution.

Paul has told of a series of extraordinary meetings he has had with former Muslims who have converted to Christ through a supernatural revelation. When two sisters saw a note on a telegraph pole advertising a 'Christian meeting and healings', they went along and witnessed the blind seeing and the lame walking. Discovering that such miracles were authenticated in the Bible, they asked their family what the Koran said about them. But they were threatened with sulphuric acid instead, and managed to escape to a 'safe-house' run by Christians. One of the women, whose name we are withholding for her protection, told of a subsequent encounter with Jesus himself. "I was sitting on my bed and Jesus came and sat next to me."

Paul said: "I have absolutely no reason to dispute what she said because of the love and joy that shone from her eyes." The leader of this safe-house, in a Middle Eastern country, was asked what he would do if the police came (it is illegal for Muslims to convert to Christianity in many Islamic countries). And he stretched out his arms, saying: "They would take me first."

Another family who experienced the miraculous deliverance of their daughter from demon possession when they turned to Jesus (Isa in the Koran) subsequently found their house bathed with light even though the shutters were down to keep out the bright sun. "And when they opened the Bible the room filled with light."

Paul went on: "God is revealing himself to Muslims in miraculous and dynamic ways. In one country there are hundreds of mullahs who have turned to Christ. And the government is really afraid of the youth there because so many have turned to Jesus. God is working in the Muslim world, appearing to people in their thousands in dreams and visions and personal visitations."

But they face terrible persecution. Another Middle Eastern convert was given 30 seconds to leave his house by his own father, or else he would be killed. Paul said that even Christians in Britain are being persecuted, particularly those from a Muslim background. He explained: "Jews and Christians are seen as lesser mortals in the eyes of Muslims – even their testimony in court counts for less – and these converts have forsaken absolutely everything for the gospel." He also told of over 2,000 Christians in a North African country who are locked up in metal containers where they virtually cook by day and freeze by night. "Many die in there rather than renounce their faith."

Another North African nation has launched a big crackdown on Christians, witnessed by a visitor whose handbag was searched for Christian literature, and yet there is a huge revival of believers in other parts of that country. "The New Testament was written for persecuted Christians," said Paul. "They faced death every day. And it's just amazing to see the joy of Christians in the same position today. They expect to be persecuted."

In North Korea believers have to make do with mouthing praise together as they sit on park benches. And in China, where millions of Christians are being persecuted, Open Doors have launched a special appeal for earthquake victims – many churches have been demolished and homes wrecked. And in a bid to encourage Christians to pray for their persecuted fellow believers, he told the story of a man who was left to freeze to death as a result of broken windows in his prison cell under Romania's old Communist regime. But God awoke believers in the West to pray for him. He was indeed freezing to death but was suddenly "strangely warmed" and, when the guards came next morning expecting to find him dead, his temperature was normal!

"I'm asking you today to stand side by side with Christians who face persecution," Paul urged a North Nottinghamshire congregation. "If one part of the body (of Christ) suffers, we all suffer."

And yet with all the evidence there is of the persecution of believers in the

Muslim world, we have an ever-increasing amount of instances in supposedly fair-minded Britain of judicial and other discrimination against Christians in favour of Islam, homosexuals and the like.

To find out more about Open Doors, visit their website at *http://www.opendoorsuk.org*

CHAPTER 13

Two states no solution

...but peace for Israel <u>will</u> come in two stages

The emphasis on alleged injustices perpetrated by Israel – highlighted by a UN-sponsored anti-racism conference in Geneva – came at a time of ongoing pressure, both from the European Union and the American administration under President Obama, for a so-called 'Two-State Solution' in which a Palestinian state would exist side by side with Israel.

But the question has to be asked as to why it is top of the agenda when there are so many other pressing international issues including the ongoing instability of Iraq, Pakistan, Afghanistan, North Korea, Iran, Syria and North Africa. And what about the starving millions in Africa, especially in beleaguered Zimbabwe, or even the dire economic crisis that affects us all? And there is even 'climate change', which so many consider the ultimate potential disaster.

What is so urgent about carving up more land that was rightfully and legally set up by a United Nations vote in the first place? Whatever it is, keeping it at the top of the agenda depends upon ongoing sympathy for the cause of the Palestinians, and so the anti-Israel media keep stoking the fires with endless stories to have you believe the Jews are the bullies rather than the victims.

The Israelis have come under much fire for alleged war crimes committed during the recent Gaza conflict with the general consensus among the world's politicians being that they used a disproportionate amount of force. But this flies in the face of the truth, which is that rockets were launched into Israel from Gaza for years (since 2002), terrorising and traumatising its citizens in the process.

If Israel was guilty of acting disproportionately, it was that for years it did nothing at all – in the interests of living at peace with its neighbours and not provoking further violence. It was disproportionate patience if anything, waiting an incredible length of time before deciding to defend its homes. Not only that, but it also compromised its military edge by warning Hamas where they were going to hit, urging families to vacate targets. Had Hamas afforded innocent Israelis the same decency? Of course not… How disproportionate!

Meanwhile the EU has threatened Israel with "dire consequences" if it does not agree to the 'two-state solution'. And though America is also pushing for it, this isn't just President Obama's initiative as his predecessor George Bush had been hoping to get agreement on this before he left office.

But the Israeli government under Benjamin Netanyahu is not likely to bow easily to such pressure. Mr Netanyahu is profoundly aware of his country's ancient heritage under God; that they are living in the 'Promised Land' which is rightfully theirs by divine decree as well as by international agreement in the 20th century. Ancient prophets like Jeremiah and Ezekiel predicted a re-gathering of the Jews after they had been scattered among the nations – neither event having yet taken place. Sure enough, after Jerusalem was destroyed by the Romans in 70 AD, the Jews were dispersed throughout the nations, as predicted. And the word of the prophet stood the test of time through the centuries, with Ezekiel writing: "Therefore say: 'This is what the Sovereign Lord says: I will gather you from the nations and bring you back from the countries where you have been scattered, and I will give you back the land of Israel again.' "

And this is exactly what has happened with Israel becoming a nation once again in 1948 – in fact three million Jews have returned to the land from more than 100 countries since then. And they have come from the north, south, east and west, just as Isaiah foretold. So why are they being pressured to give up what is rightfully theirs – both in the providence of God and by international agreement?

And will it make a jot of difference if they do? Will there be peace in the Middle East? Not likely because, as Israel's politicians argue, it will only serve to provide a launching pad for terrorism right on the doorstep of their capital and, in any case, Hamas (not to mention Iran) have no intention of living at peace with Israel as neighbours. They don't believe they have a right to any of the land they currently occupy. And as for Iran, they have made it plain that they wish Israel "wiped off the map" altogether.

A two-state solution, therefore, is no solution. How about looking to God's solution, clearly outlined in the Bible with a perfect plan for every individual and nation?

As St Paul wrote to the Colossians, "Here (in receiving the Spirit of Christ) there is neither Greek nor Jew, circumcised nor uncircumcised, barbarian,

Scythian, slave or free, but Christ is all, and is in all."

Actually, the ancient predictions of the prophets have a double application in that Israel's restoration is seen as a 'two-stage solution', so to speak. In other words, it would be both physical and spiritual. For the seers foretold that, sometime after they were re-gathered to the Promised Land, the Jews as a whole would at last recognise their Messiah – "the one whom they had pierced" (Zechariah) – at which point they foresaw a mass return to the God of their fathers. (Such a move is already gathering pace). And the Second Coming of Christ, the Prince of Peace, would finally end centuries of conflict. Come, Lord Jesus!

A 'Two-State Solution' would see the Palestinians established alongside Israel as part of the 'road map' to peace. But Mr Netanyahu does not believe in a divided capital of Jerusalem – for practical as well as religious reasons – and is not likely to succumb too easily to American pressure, especially with having to consider the demands of the ultra-orthodox Shas Party.

The U.S. leaders, in an apparent attempt to appease aggressive Muslim states, believe that the only prospect of peace lies with Israel accepting this 'solution' in return for support over the potential nuclear threat of Iran. But would that be enough, bearing in mind that Israel is surrounded by enemies wishing their demise? One commentator said: "Israel is being backed into a corner in order to allow the U.S. to solidify ties with the Arab countries which surround it."

Iran does indeed appear to be in an advanced state of nuclear readiness, but at the same time Israel's anti-missile system has been successfully tested – jointly conducted, it is understood, with the American missile defence agency. It's a heady mix that amounts to a potentially apocalyptic situation. Jesus himself predicted a time of great distress – especially in the Middle East – immediately preceding his Second Coming. And we could well be very close to that scenario. Even a non-religious Jew, a South African dentist working in Israel, has said: "There are many Jews today that feel we live in the days of the Mashiach (Messiah). Time will tell. Big changes may be on the way and could affect all the world. I only hope they are for the good."

And Christian journalist David Dolan, who has lived in Israel for 25 years, has this to say: "With increasingly strong shockwaves engulfing the region and the world, it appears that the time when Israel's Messiah will reign in glory from Jerusalem is drawing very close." Referring to this period, Jesus said that "unless those days were shortened, no flesh would survive."

Complicating the whole issue is the fact that the Shas are fanatically opposed to Messianic believers – the fast-growing body of Jews (both in Israel and around the world) who believe that Jesus is the Messiah. And then there is the growth of those within the church who don't believe God has a special plan for the Jews, but rather that the Church has replaced them as the 'apple of his eye' because of their rejection of the Christ.

This is complete nonsense, of course, as for one thing the entire early church was made up of Jews and, in fulfilment of ancient prophecies, a growing number of Jews are now acknowledging Jesus (Yeshua) as their Messiah. The Bible is clear from beginning to end – God has a special plan for Jews, who are also to be a blessing to the Gentiles.

And then there was the denunciation of Israel by the majority of those attending the Durban II Conference in Geneva despite a walkout by Western diplomats during an anti-Semitic speech by Iran's President Ahmadinejad. The initial hosts of this so-called anti-racism conference were Durban, South Africa – and I noticed that, on BBC television, a prominent anti-apartheid campaigner claimed that Israel had supported the apartheid state.

This is an example of the many ridiculous claims about Israel that bear no relation to the truth – in South Africa's case it was in fact Jews who were at the forefront of the fight against apartheid. And most notable among them was the indefatigable Helen Suzman, who fought alone for decades in the Cape Parliament to bring down an unjust system based on race. She succeeded, Nelson Mandela was released and the rest is history. Actually, the Jews by and large support a just and fair society – and this should not be surprising considering they come from the same race as our Lord Jesus Christ!

CHAPTER 14

Israel, a sign of the Second Coming

The combination of an earthquake of unprecedented force striking Chile with the simultaneous escalation of war-mongering in the Middle East – as happened recently – should act as a wake-up call to those who fail to see that we are facing an apocalypse. All the signs indicating the imminent return of Christ are there for all to see. In particular, Jesus spoke of an increase in wars, famines, plagues and earthquakes, comparing the latter with the labour pains of a woman, i.e. that the contractions would be more frequent and the pain more severe as the birth of the baby drew closer. The Chilean 'quake, registering 8.8 on the Richter scale, came hot on the heels of a similar one in Haiti which all but destroyed that island.

Another key sign of the end is the worldwide persecution of Israel. Perhaps distracted by conflicts elsewhere on the one hand, and a continuing obsession with our favourite TV soap opera on the other, we failed to recognise that the clouds of war on an even bigger scale are gathering over the Middle East. And it could affect the whole world, with Britain and the United States also drawn in, making them vulnerable to further fearful internal attacks.

The nation of Israel – the focus of such a conflagration – is facing a double whammy. One the one hand her sworn enemy Iran, already supplying rockets and missiles to terrorist groups Hamas and Hezbollah to fire at the state, is also rapidly reaching the point of being able to build a nuclear weapon for the purpose of fulfilling an oft-repeated declaration of their president to "wipe Israel off the map".

On the other hand the world's most powerful nations – represented by the so-called Quartet of America, Russia, the EU and the UN – are putting pressure on Israel to agree to a Palestinian state with East Jerusalem as its capital. The Bible declares that those who bless Israel will themselves be blessed, but that those who belittle them will be cursed, which goes some way to explaining why Britain is experiencing such turmoil at present. As already discussed, dividing the land God promised his chosen people in ancient days is seen as particularly galling to the Almighty and it seems the nations are sparing no effort to rob Israel of what little land she has.

And the BBC, already reprimanded for its bias over Israel, stoked up the fire with a documentary designed to depict how ruthless the nation is by their eviction of an Arab family in Jerusalem. But they gave no explanation of the background to the situation – the fact that the house in question was owned by Jews from before 1948, that the Arab family living there since 1967 knew they had to pay rent and it was their failure to do so that resulted in eviction.

According to Middle East expert Lance Lambert, the Quartet are on a "direct collision course with God Almighty" with their current pressure on Israel, inviting judgment compared with which the ten plagues of Egypt would be as child's play. Some of this is already apparent with the financial chaos into which the Eurozone have sunk. "The worst is yet to come for Britain and the United States," added the Israel-based author and speaker who has a special insight into biblical prophecy and how it relates to the Middle East. "Their determination to divide the Promised Land can only result in disaster."

He compared their predicament to that of the Babylonian empire under King Nebuchadnezzar which had been weighed in the balance and found wanting and would disappear in one night. "In particular the UK has a bleak future," he went on, noting the way in which Muslims have virtually taken over some British cities. He warned: "Militant Islam is determined to take over the world – in particular the Western nations with their Christian past."

And I should add here that we have opened the door to this not only through our immigration policies but with the way in which, while the Asian population grows apace in the normal way, indigenous citizens have been seduced into either avoiding having babies through contraception or killing them in the womb if they are conceived. "The sun is setting on Great Britain," Lambert added, with its anti-Semitism, boycotting of Israeli goods and its misrepresentation of Israel by its national broadcasting corporation. "The Almighty who made Britain great (a nation which ruled more than a quarter of our planet just 70 years ago) has finally turned his back on her."

What's more, the triangle of states encompassing Afghanistan, Pakistan and Iran could result not only in the final eclipse of Britain and America, but also plunge the entire globe into World War III. We are talking of a battle for the control of the nations, he said, which Islam had tried twice before in human history – in 732 and 1683 – and only failed at the last minute through Christians emboldened by the Spirit of God. Current negotiations designed to help bring about a Middle East settlement were forecast by Old Testament writers who predicted a time when false prophets would talk of "peace, peace, when there is no peace".

Lambert went on: "We're being seduced by peace plans that appeal to the Israeli people – I know nobody who doesn't long for peace in Israel." But he warned of the fearful prospect of a cataclysmic war foretold by the prophet Ezekiel some 2,600 years ago that seems to have something to do with Russia and Iran. "There really will be no peace until the Prince of Peace (Jesus Christ) comes. And those who come against Jerusalem will be bankrupted and destroyed." And he spoke of the growing realisation among leaders in Israel that evangelical Christians (though unfortunately not all of them) are the only friends Israel has. "The only real answer to Israel is a spiritual awakening. We need the Messiah as much as anyone else does."

Meanwhile Dr Michael Evans of the Jerusalem Prayer Team, which campaigns on Israel's behalf, warns:

"This is a crucial moment in Israel's history. Her enemies gather like ravenous wolves circling their prey, constantly plotting and working toward her destruction. The world community is either turning a blind eye to the (nuclear) threat or actively helping Iran acquire these weapons of mass destruction. …This is more than a political or military struggle – this is a spiritual battle. The enemy wants control of Jerusalem because the Holy City is central to God's prophetic plan for the future of our world."

So what have Israel done to deserve their present predicament, you may well ask? A brief but wholly inadequate explanation is that they are the target of jealousy built up over millennia because they claim, and are seen, to be a people specially chosen by God. How do you explain the logic of a nation – re-born following World War II partly out of sympathy for their persecution by the Nazis – now still the target of vicious anti-Semitism? And how is it that the Quartet of powerful nations are pressurising them to divide their land still further in order to make peace?

It was Churchill who, at the stroke of a pen, reduced the extent of the land promised by the League of Nations (the forerunner to the UN) in 1920 by more than three-quarters. And the United Nations subsequently further reduced the proposed Jewish homeland to three small pockets, each joined by a single road – a country smaller than South Africa's famous Kruger National Park reserved for wildlife!

To conclude, a great conflict in the Middle East along with hostility towards Israel from all nations is among the key signs that we are in the final days of this age, according to the Bible. And the fact that another of the signs, the restoration of Israel as a Jewish homeland, has already taken place a generation ago, suggests that the curtain could soon come down on the present dispensation, ushering in the glorious return of Christ to rule and reign from Jerusalem for a thousand years of perfect peace. The final pieces of the jigsaw are falling into place. It isn't a pretty picture now, and won't be for those who have disowned Christ or cursed Israel. But when all is as it should be, and judgment has fallen on evil politicians and others who have defied God, the world will indeed be the beautiful place it was designed to be.

Iranian leader prays for Islamic 'messiah'

Christians and all fair-minded people should be rallying to the cause of Israel, especially in the light of the inflammatory 2010 speech to the United Nations General Assembly by Iran's President Ahmadinejad during which – on American soil – he began by praying for Allah to hasten the arrival of the Imam al-Mahdi, an Islamic 'messiah' whom Shia Muslims believe will come at the end of days to destroy Judeo-Christian civilization, force 'infidels' to convert and set up a one-world Islamic government known as the 'caliphate'. And the Iranian leader believes the way to hasten his coming is to annihilate Israel and the United States.

New York Times best-selling author Joel Rosenberg asks what we should do in response to all this. "We need to get ready and be prepared," he said, adding that we need to pray for the peace of Jerusalem, stand with Israel, care for poor and needy Israelis and Palestinians, stockpile humanitarian relief supplies and build the infrastructure to distribute even more emergency aid when the next war comes. "And we need to show that Jesus Christ is the Prince of Peace and the only hope of reconciliation."

These are, indeed, the last days, judging by the many signs Jesus predicted as indicating the imminence of his return. But though President Ahmadinejad's provocation may well hasten the approach of an Armageddon scenario as described in the Book of Revelation, his vision of a victory over Christ is entirely misplaced. Jesus is coming – this time not as a baby in a manger but as King of Kings – to set up his rule on earth so that "every knee will bow and every tongue confess that Jesus is Lord" as the Bible foretells.

Politicians repeatedly pressure Israel into carving up its territory and pulling back from areas like Gaza and Lebanon as a means of securing peace, and it's the same over the push for a Palestinian state. But all that followed previous withdrawals was more rocket-fire and terror. True harmony will only be achieved through the Prince of Peace when he comes to reign. The politics of the Middle East, which has a constant knock-on effect on the rest of the world, is the real good v evil scenario that Christians and others should take on board – prayerfully, and with action if possible, through political and practical support.

Peace talks precede Armageddon

With Iran about to go nuclear and a pre-emptive strike on its facilities by Israel a distinct possibility, it would seem that the world is on the brink of Armageddon. Peace talks are re-started on a seemingly constant basis. I saw a notice in a Quaker meeting house advertising a group for people searching for peace. And for a Christian movement that began with heavenly-minded fire, the notice spoke somewhat strangely of 'earth-focused' peace – whatever that is; perhaps reflecting an eco-friendly ethos.

The quest for peace is a laudable aspiration, but the answer won't be found in man-made efforts, either on the small scale of the Quaker meeting or on the bigger canvas of Middle East talks. The Bible itself speaks of false prophets who soothe us with words of 'peace, peace' when there is no peace. There are realities we first have to face – key among them being that a catastrophic war is imminent and no amount of nonsense talk about peace (often at any price) will avert disaster. The devil is not in the business of making peace treaties, and when we realise the inevitability of a battle that must be fought, we can look for – and find – a peaceful path through the storm. This is all about the foundation on which we choose to build our lives. Jesus said that if we build on sand, the storms of life would wash us away, but that if we build our lives on him (the Rock), we will always stand firm, even in the face of hurricanes from hell, and we would come to know true peace "beyond all understanding".

Back to the imminence of war, a shipment of nuclear fuel is probably being loaded into the core of Tehran's first Bushehr reactor as I write. Iran, of course, continues to insist that their plant is being built to provide electricity but has made no secret of its desire to destroy Israel. Armageddon (the plain of Megiddo in Israel) is a real place of which the Bible (in the Book of Revelation) foretells of an apocalyptic end-time battle that will take place there when all the nations of the earth come against Israel. Such a scenario could well follow a pre-emptive strike on Iran with much of the world (even including America) now turned against Israel and believing the Islamic-inspired lie that Jews and Christians are behind all the world's problems, with Israel painted as the bully rather than the victim.

At the same time Western nations have largely discarded the Christian heritage that has made them the success they are, and have thus lost their connection and understanding with God's ancient people without whom we would have neither the Scriptures, nor Jesus, nor many of the world's great men, nor even civilization itself. We have truly lost our way and God has vowed to judge the nations according to how they have treated his people, the Jews.

With all this in mind, where do we stand? Are we on the rock with Jesus and his people, or are we on sinking sand in a world where even the financial power-houses of the West are collapsing all around us?

In 2010 we heard of a mega-mosque planned for Ground Zero, in the shadow of the Twin Towers brought down by Islamic terrorists on 9/11. And to add insult to injury, construction was set to commence on September 11, 2011, exactly ten years after the terrifying attack. The Islamic world is making a mockery of the West. Republican presidential candidate Newt Gingrich likened the mosque to raising a swastika at a Holocaust memorial, or a Japanese cultural centre at Pearl Harbour. "You can build a mosque at Ground Zero when we can build a synagogue in Mecca," said one banner at a huge protest held in New York. Daily Mail columnist Richard Littlejohn said it was difficult not to conclude that the location of this project was deliberately designed to be provocative. And it was said that most of its cost would be funded from Saudi Arabia, who would never allow a Christian church to be built in Riyadh.

With Armageddon thus a very real prospect, whose side are you on? Is your future hope and present peace built on the Rock that is Christ, or on the sinking sand of materialism and secular humanism with the rest of mankind? Weigh up the reality, and decide where you stand.

A Prince of Peace for the Middle East

Meanwhile the BBC came under intense fire for refusing to broadcast a charity appeal to help the victims of the war in Gaza – several of its rivals had agreed to air the plea, although Sky TV decided to follow the BBC's example. The BBC's position was that they did not wish to be seen as taking sides in a conflict which is immensely complicated and about which it is not at all clear who is to blame for what. Already accused by media watchdogs of anti-Israel bias, the 'Beeb' were clearly attempting to redress this perception of their stance and were therefore in a no-win situation.

On top of which they were worried at the time about the effects of a certain overpaid presenter, Jonathan Ross, who had taken up where he left off when he began a three-month suspension for appalling behaviour on a radio show. Determined to stick with his four-letter word mantra and referring to those who wish him silenced as part of a "brave new world", Ross re-launched his career with further expletives along with an obscene sexual reference to an 80-year-old woman apparently suffering from Alzheimer's.

The spill-over of the Middle East conflict into British society is evident with many joining in public protests in support of Palestinians – those they see as victims – while others see things differently. The truth is that everyone living in that part of the world – both Jew and Arab – during the British mandate from 1917-1948 were regarded as Palestinians and the land now occupied by Israel is but a fraction of what they were promised, both from the international community and from God himself in the scriptures!

Most Jews do not believe they occupy Palestinian land. It is theirs by right of ancient promises, and the Arabs who were there when the modern Jewish state was born were not expelled, as some historians suggest, but encouraged to stay while neighbouring Arab nations urged them to flee without being prepared to accommodate them, thus creating an artificial refugee crisis which could be used to milk sympathy for an 'anti-Jewish' cause.

The Middle East conflict has even spread to the church as for the past several decades it has been divided along the lines of those who believe God has not forsaken his chosen people and those who believe the Church has replaced the Jews in God's plans... that somehow, because the Jews rejected Jesus when he came (though in fact the early church was almost entirely Jewish), God has not felt obliged to keep his promise to restore them to himself. But this goes against the very nature of God, who will never break his word, and the scriptures speak clearly of a time when the Jews scattered throughout the nations will return to the Promised Land, and that this physical re-birth will be followed in due course by a spiritual re-birth when they will recognise their Messiah. And even as I write there are up to 25,000 Jews living in Israel who believe Yeshua (Jesus) is their Messiah. Peace in the Middle East and peace in the Church are possible only through the reconciling spirit of the Prince of Peace, Jesus Christ.

CHAPTER 15

The stark choice
facing Britain

On the day we marked the fourth anniversary of the 7/7 bombings in London, we were told that the capital's transport network was still vulnerable to terrorist attack. The occasion was marked by the unveiling of a poignant memorial to the 52 victims in Hyde Park although there were, of course, also hundreds wounded on that fateful day, including my own brother.

The tragedy is that, instead of the threat of a possible Islamic takeover of Britain receding as a result of the revulsion against such terrible outrage, it has probably increased as appeasement, rather than counter-attack, has become the norm. Leading British journalist Peter Hitchens, for one, said he believed Britain could soon become a Muslim country because Christianity here is too feeble. Hitchens, an Anglican, was concerned that the Christian religion on which British society is based is "constantly trashed", and told London's Premier Radio: "Islam has the strength and will eventually also have the numbers to become dominant. That will change Britain in many, many different ways and people who want to drive Christianity out should work out now which one of those they prefer because if they don't get one, they will get the other."

He is right; this is the stark choice. Do British people want a Muslim state, or would they prefer to go back to their Christian roots and save themselves from disaster? "You can wear the veil as a Muslim but you can't wear a cross," Hitchens pointed out (though a Catholic school in Blackburn swam against the tide by banning – for security reasons – a visiting Muslim teacher for wearing a veil. The school said it was operating a strict policy where guests must be identified.) Hitchens continued: "The whole thing is ludicrous and needs turning on its head. The Church needs to say, 'No, we are Christians and this is a Christian society'." The fact is that the Muslim population has multiplied ten times faster than the rest of society, according to research by the Office for National Statistics. And in the same period, according to

Premier Radio, the number of Christians in the country fell by more than two million.

Other Christians with a more optimistic view of Britain's future include Pastor David Devenish, who suggests that the popularity of the Alpha (introduction to the faith) courses shows Christianity is growing. He sees many "signs of life" – and I do too. But we need an outright revival – a radical return to the dynamic roots of the gospel in terms of it drastically affecting our lifestyle – if we are to reverse the current trend of appeasement and political correctness.

Horrific stories paint a gruesome picture of a future United Kingdom under Islam. In Somalia, for instance, Islamic extremists beheaded two young boys because their Christian father refused to give out information about a church leader. In Iran, a strict Muslim state, British embassy officials were arrested for allegedly fomenting the riots that followed elections generally perceived to have been rigged. And in Pakistan, Christians were attacked by 500 outraged members of a Muslim mob over a blasphemy accusation against them. According to some estimates, about 100 Christian houses and churches were set on fire, with men and women tortured and the police only 'silent spectators'. Is this what the British people want, or would they prefer to return to their Christian roots based on the Bible's call to love one's neighbour?

Britain is under a curse

For those willing to wake up and smell the coffee, Britain is indeed under a curse which she has brought on herself. Moses warned the ancient Israelites that they had a choice of blessing or a curse. Obedience to the Lord's ways (summarised in the Ten Commandments) would invite blessing, demonstrated in an extension of her territory, power and respect as those who worship false gods are driven out of national influence. But a curse would result from turning away from the Lord's commands by following other gods "which you have not known".

The whole stark choice (and national outcome) is centred on worship – whether true or false. And as most people will acknowledge, Britain has largely forsaken her Christian heritage with the government and media leading the way. And we are reaping the rotten harvest that has resulted from this "famine" of godly instruction and are cursed specifically through failing to bless Israel. It may be politically incorrect to say so, but no longer as a nation do we worship the God of our fathers, who extended our territory until it straddled the globe as an empire upon which the sun never set.

The God of our fathers caused great men like William Wilberforce to fight throughout his parliamentary career for an end to slavery; David Livingstone to exchange the comfortable existence of being a doctor in Scotland for a disease-ridden Africa in order to preach the gospel to those who hadn't heard it; and Olympic gold medallist Eric Liddell to die in China as a relatively young man because of his love for Jesus Christ. But now we worship other gods – humanism, secularism and atheism in particular among the ruling elite. And some of us are turning to outright paganism and witchcraft, supported by the establishment. Hertfordshire Police, for example, even went as far as appointing two pagan chaplains. And we were told, in their defence, that witchcraft is not the hocus-pocus, puff of smoke, turning-people-into-frogs stuff you see on television, but "working with nature for good".

That just about sums up where we are today – in the middle of an environmentally-friendly, 'green god' situation in which we find ourselves worshipping created things rather than the Creator. But we were meant to rule over creation, not be subservient to it, and worship the Creator, not the created.

The day Hitler missed the boat

The calling of a national day of prayer in Britain a few years ago was a welcome move from the churches – it was just a shame that the Coalition Government, for politically correct reasons no doubt, couldn't have reinforced the call with its own backing. The Nigerian Government, in recognising that their nation is in trouble, had shown that this could, and should, be done. President Goodluck Jonathan, in acknowledging the need for God's guidance, said "the way out of the challenges facing the country" was through trust in God, adding that he could not succeed without divine help.

And with the current recession threatening to sink our own economy, we are reminded of a time when these islands faced the threat of invasion from Nazi Germany, and our freedom was within a flicker of being snatched from our grasp. Fortunately King George VI, with the support of Prime Minister Churchill, recognised our dependence on God and called the nation to prayer. This was followed by the miraculous rescue of 335,000 Allied soldiers from the beaches of Dunkirk, and the subsequent turnaround of our fortunes in World War II. The atheist Hitler had missed the boat(s) as Christian England turned to their Saviour. (Though nominally Catholic, Hitler was in fact virulently anti-Christianity, seeking his guidance from horoscopes and the occult in general).

And we are probably in more peril now than then. The dark forces of atheism that would have held us in its icy grip had Hitler succeeded have nevertheless infiltrated the major institutions – Parliament, the media and even some sections of the church. And Islam, which would have non-adherents in submission to its harsh tenets given half the chance, is in the ascendancy all over Europe, threatening our freedom and future as much as

National Socialism ever did. And no-one with the authority and gravitas of Mr Churchill is raising his voice to alert us to the danger. We are riding a storm from which only He who walked on water can rescue us.

We are encouraged, however, that there are prayer movements in this country, supported by intercessors from South Korea and inspired by the annual Global Day of Prayer which originated in South Africa just a few years ago. Korea is bathed in Christian revival with huge congregations all over the country and the momentum of this spiritual awakening has been kept up through continuous prayer in churches and special retreats. The South Africans also know something about how revival is wrought through prayer, especially through the legacy of 19th century revivalist Andrew Murray, through whose family my orphaned great-grandfather was nurtured in the Christian faith. And more recently that country has been indebted to the ministry of farmer Angus Buchan, who has drawn hundreds of thousands of men to his KwaZulu-Natal farm for a series of conferences on living for Christ.

So what is prayer? It is asking God for help; it is involving him in our lives; it is demonstrating our dependency on him. Jesus taught us to do this through a pattern known as the Lord's Prayer which includes asking our Father for our daily bread and asking him to forgive us as we forgive others! Prayer also develops our faith because every time we receive a tangible answer, it strengthens our trust in our heavenly Father. People often say to me, "I wish I had your faith!" But faith isn't something that falls out of the sky, like some angelic gift. Well, there is a glimmer of truth in that because it is a gift from God. But everyone can develop a strong faith simply by starting where they are and exercising the little faith they have. For example, ask God for a parking space next time you go shopping in a busy town centre. Then ask him to heal your toothache; and gradually work up to bigger things.

Prayer can even have mental health benefits, according to psychiatry professor Andrew Newberg in a new book based on recent research. Declaring that prayer has concentrating and calming effects, he said scans showed that a region of the brain that focuses the mind and fosters compassion is stimulated during prayer while those parts linked to fear and anger are calmed. And separate research has shown that church services lower your blood pressure. Torgeir Sorensen, from the School of Theology and Religious Psychology Centre in Norway, said: "We found that the more often the participants went to church the lower their blood pressure."

Some people take a giant leap of faith right at the start of their Christian lives because they have taken up the challenge I often suggest to those who may be searching for answers – they have dared to make a really big request by asking God to reveal himself. And if this is done with sincerity, the resulting divine encounter gets new believers racing out of the starting blocks. And when you've realised that God can change your life, you'll know he can change the nation too.

Thinking of the Japanese surrender in August 1945, which followed the horrific effects of the atomic bombs dropped on Hiroshima and Nagasaki, let's not wait (either as individuals or as a nation) until our world is blown apart either by circumstances or compromise with evil forces. Isn't it time we raised the white flag of surrender to God, and turned to him in prayer?

CHAPTER 16

The Challenge to Israel

Another 'Red Sea Crossing'

Threatened with another holocaust at the hands of implacable enemies on all sides, Israelis have been turning to God in prayer – and it seems to be working.

While the world's media pointed to the huge discrepancy in the number of war dead resulting from a recent conflict as indicative of a 'disproportionate' response to rocket attacks from Gaza, Israelis hailed it as a miraculous deliverance reminiscent of the escape from Egypt across the Red Sea. The official death toll was something like 1,300 on the side of Hamas (which included many Palestinians either caught in the crossfire or because they were used as 'human shields' to invoke sympathy for the Hamas cause) and just 13 Israelis – a ratio of 100-1.

As one Israeli pointed out, this is partly because his country built a strong army in the knowledge that they couldn't rely on the support of the West against their aggressors. But in a remarkable report from inside Israel, an unnamed Jewish lady has talked of "amazing miracles of protection and divine direction" during the battle and of "an astonishing spiritual awakening as a result of this conflict".

Jews were joining together in prayer to the Almighty as they felt once again threatened with extinction – as they had been in ancient times under Haman, more recently under Hitler and now by Hamas. When Esther, the Persian Queen, discovered that Haman, a royal official, desired to perpetrate genocide against her people, the Jews, her uncle Mordecai challenged her to implore the king to intervene. And when she did, the plan for the destruction of the Jews was thwarted and Esther's people were allowed to live in peace.

Now, Israeli soldiers were going into battle wearing tzitzit (prayer tassles) and carrying the Book of Psalms while tent synagogues on the battlefield had at least ten sessions every morning. Among incidents of divine deliverance cited were how a rocket completely destroyed an empty kindergarten after the Mayor of Beersheva felt he should cancel school that day. And of how a soldier who had moved to Israel from England less than two years earlier was thrown into the air by an explosion, but only needed stitches even after a piece of shrapnel penetrated his entire neck, somehow missing his main artery, vein and spinal cord by millimetres.

Our correspondent was upset that only negative propaganda from the terrorists was reported by the media in a bid to make Israel look like blood-thirsty killers. "One has to grieve over the terrible destruction of the cities of Gaza and the horrific human tragedy going on there, but the responsibility for the suffering and death is directly on the doorstep of the Hamas leadership. These deluded people think that their god, Allah, will give them victory, and have entered into a battle with the true Holy One of Abraham, Isaac and Jacob that they will never win."

She adds: "We are becoming increasingly aware that a greater power than us is on our side… The rest of the nations have not remembered the threats of Hitler, and how the Jewish people were almost wiped out because no-one wanted to believe he actually meant what he said. Contrary to those who want to hide their heads in the sands of political correctness, there is a right and a wrong side in this conflict. It is a battle between darkness and light."

But threats to Israel are not restricted to their immediate neighbours. Even as I write awful incidents of anti-Semitism are reported from France while, closer to home, in the north London suburb of Golders Green, the Jewish community have become increasingly security conscious following threats to their safety as a blind world continues to insist on seeing Israel as the aggressor rather than the victim. But the God of Israel has promised to keep his people from all harm and watch over their lives (Psalm 121) and it is also foretold (in the Book of Zechariah) that the Jewish people would in the 'last days' turn to their Messiah en masse because of their trouble. That time, it seems, has almost come.

…But Israel needs to trust in the Lord!

We've talked about how Israel has been spared time and again as enemies who threatened to overwhelm them were suddenly turned back, probably through God's personal intervention since they are his chosen people. But they can't forever rely on God to bail them out when they continually refuse to trust and be dependent on him, as the prophets make clear. Warning that they will lose their inheritance and be enslaved to their enemies because of their sin, Jeremiah writes: "This is what the Lord says: 'Cursed is the one who trusts in man, who depends on flesh for his strength and whose heart turns away from the Lord.' (Jeremiah 17.5)"

And Hosea explores a similar theme – that Israel needs to trust the Lord, not rely on its military. Their patriarch Joshua was a brilliant military leader who, in the period covered by the book named after him, defeated a total of 31 armies as well as capturing a great many cities. And the secret of his success was that he evidently obeyed the instruction given to him by the Lord to "meditate on (the Book of the Law) day and night… for then you will be prosperous and successful." (Joshua 1.8)

And where is the spirit of David, who challenged Goliath with the words: "You come against me with sword and spear and javelin, but I come against you in the name of the Lord Almighty, the God of the armies of Israel, whom you have defied"? Tragically, the blight of secularism has also infected Israel, God's chosen people, who have found themselves caught up in a worldwide phenomenon which, despite having been thoroughly discredited and exposed for the bitter fruit it produces by the effects of Communism, has recently enjoyed a revival, especially in the former heartland of Christian (Western) civilization.

Britain bedevilled by atheism

Yes, the Berlin Wall may have come down in 1989, but the heart of Communist ideology has found a new home.

As the swinging sixties gave a gyrating young generation a new sense of 'freedom' in the West (if casting off restraint can be classed as freedom), the menacing chains of Communism cranked up their vice-like grip in the East. And among those at the sharp end was a Romanian pastor called Richard Wurmbrand, who spent 14 years in prison for his Christian faith, three of them in solitary confinement. Wurmbrand, a Jew and former atheist, finally reached the West where he became a key spokesman for the dreadful suffering of the 'Underground Church' in the Soviet Union and the Communist bloc as a whole.

An updated version of his story, *Tortured for Christ*, was published a few years ago to mark the 40th anniversary of Release International, the charity he founded as the voice of persecuted Christians. And while acknowledging that the Iron Curtain had come down, the point is emphasised that persecution continues in many of the former Communist countries – as of course it does in Communist China, North Korea and all over the Muslim world. The tragedy is that in the 24 years since the fall of the Berlin Wall, the atheism and humanism that is at the heart of Communist ideology has found a new home in Britain and other Western countries where much of the mainstream media and political elite have hijacked the anti-God dogma disguised as intelligent thinking.

A nation established on biblical principles has cut itself off from its roots and is floating downstream on a hopeless tide driven by hatred of Christianity. The Christian voice is crushed at every opportunity, though thankfully there are some lone voices in the wilderness – like our Queen – courageously standing for truth. Murder, mayhem and sexual immorality is legalised and encouraged by government while those calling for purity are demonised as fascists or worse. Millions of unborn babies have been murdered in their mothers' wombs, all-night drinking was given the Parliamentary seal of approval (though it failed miserably to deal with the chaos on our streets caused by drunken yobs) and the gay agenda is backed to the hilt by every level of government so that even a pensioner is harassed by police for objecting to it.

Wurmbrand in his book stresses time and again the connection between the poison of atheism and the sort of brute Neanderthal aggression he himself experienced in prison simply because he refused to deny his beliefs. The simple proclamation that Christ had died for our sins and had risen from the dead was sufficient to bring down the jackboot brutality that left him bruised and beaten almost to a pulp so that it was a miracle he survived. He was beaten on the soles of his feet and once repeatedly thrown into a fridge where, just as he was about to freeze to death, the guards would retrieve him and thaw him out, only to put him back in again. Others were tortured with red-hot irons and endured many more unspeakable atrocities.

One Christian man had to endure the sight of his 14-year-old son being whipped and beaten to death with blood spattered across the prison cell. He even decided to give in to his tormentors as he couldn't bear to see the boy suffering any longer, but his son – Alexander – refused, saying: "Father, don't do me the injustice of having a traitor as a parent. Withstand! If they kill me, I will die with the words, 'Jesus and my fatherland'." The enraged Communists finished him off, but the boy died praising God. His father, however, was never the same again.

Despite the brutality, Wurmbrand and other Christians continued to love their torturers, so much so that many leading Communists became Christians – and this in itself is what contributed to the fall of Communism in Europe. With stories like these, Communism is now discredited, but has been resurrected on these shores in another form – with its partner-in-crime atheism now in vogue among the intelligentsia. And it was also exhumed in the form of the new 'United States of Europe' under the Treaty of Lisbon, with secular/atheistic laws and tendencies remarkably similar to those of the old Soviet bloc.

Jesus explained that when a demon-possessed person is exorcised, a vacuum is left that needs to be filled with the goodness of God. If not, the demon returns and the last state of that person is worse than the first. That is what has happened both in the former USSR and Britain. In the latter case we brought down our own protecting wall of Christianity.

In a similar way there has been a revival of witchcraft in Britain since missionaries dealt with much demonic activity in Africa by freeing people from its clutches with the gospel of Christ. The restless spirits sought somewhere else to live and found a ready home in the very country which brought them Christianity. Now a nation in chaos has many of the characteristics of the old Communist states where individuality is gradually being crushed and where drunkenness and suicides are rife. And our governments have been under pressure to tackle both by making them easier.

Because of a culture of atheism, which leaves them with no purpose in life, the UK youth take to binge-drinking just as they did in the Soviet system. Judging by their reckless lifestyles and especially the way many of them drive cars, our young generation seem also to have no sense of mortality. And it is interesting that Wurmbrand encourages parents to take children to burials to help them face up to reality and learn that life is transitory. He also tells us that many Communists commit suicide, including their greatest poets and their great writer Fadeev. "He had just finished his novel called *Happiness* in which he had explained that happiness consists in working tirelessly for communism. He was so happy about it that he shot himself after having finished the novel. It was difficult for his soul to bear such a great lie."

The reason for the cruelty of the Communists, Wurmbrand argues, is that they have been brainwashed into believing there is no God, no hereafter, no judgment – no-one to whom they will ultimately have to give account. And on the issue of individuality, he writes: "They only know the masses. Their word is that of the demon in the New Testament who, when asked what his name was, replied: 'We are legion'. Individual personality – one of the great gifts of God to humankind – must be crushed."

The collectivism of Communism is raising its ugly head with political correctness marching the masses into a straitjacket of conformity in which they are no longer encouraged to think and speak for themselves. And then there is the ever-growing cesspit of immorality so much a part of Communism – particularly in the encouragement of abortion – and which is now bedevilling our society. It's not surprising that Communism and immorality go hand in hand because it cuts itself off from the God of morality!

And then there's the whole sickening area of compromise in the Church. While Christians suffer elsewhere for their faith, theologians in the West discuss trifles. And even the apparently big story around the Pope offering a welcome to disaffected Anglicans doesn't really address the issues of life and death underpinning the Christian faith. The church's compromise with the world and the spirit of the age has been a problem for millennia, and was witnessed by Wurmbrand in Eastern Europe where church leaders sold out to the Communists and betrayed their brothers. They were 'wolves in sheep's clothing' declaring that Christianity and Communism were essentially the same.

But persecution soon sorts out the sheep from the goats. Wurmbrand tells of the time when the Russians occupied Romania and two armed soldiers entered a church threatening to shoot anyone who didn't immediately abandon his faith. Those who recanted fled for their lives whereupon the soldiers embraced those remaining with the words, "We too, are Christians, but we wished to have fellowship only with those who consider the truth worth dying for."

The Underground Church, though poor and suffering, has few lukewarm members.

Sick, soulless, secularism

Secularism creates a society that is uncaring, soulless and amoral epitomised by the recent case of the child who had been twice run over and left for dead in a Chinese street as people passed by without stopping to help. I also know of a young English lady who, while teaching in Moscow, witnessed the appalling spectacle of a militiaman carelessly kicking someone sprawled on the ground to check if he was still alive. Fortunately it made her question the meaning of life and she subsequently became an ardent believer. Humanism and its total independence from God is a great danger to society and I'm afraid it has even influenced many of the anti-capitalist protestors railing against the injustice of the system by calling for transparency from politicians and financiers while wearing face-masks to protect their identity!

The trouble is that God has been thrown out of the window, to be replaced by commercialism, hedonism, frantic busy-ness and everything except what is really important. People seem to spend their entire waking lives on their mobile phones, obviously never having time just to stop and consider what life is all about, while shops are open all hours – and yet for all this we're in economic meltdown!

Thankfully, most Jews still honour the Sabbath, but that can't be said for most of us in the West. And it spells disaster. We were never meant to work seven days a week – not even the Creator of the universe did so. He created the world in six days, and then rested. Jesus made the point that the Sabbath was made for man, and not man for the Sabbath, in correcting the legalistic attitude of the religious leaders who even wanted to forbid healing on the Sabbath!

The point he was making was that it is for our good (physically, spiritually and emotionally) rather than an opportunity to win ritualistic brownie points. But if your donkey (or car) falls into a ditch, you are perfectly at liberty to rescue it. Regular rest is essential – ask any doctor – for that is how we were created, and in any case the Sabbath is the fourth of the Ten Commandments, and we need to honour our Maker. Do the shops and supermarkets make more money by opening all hours? I hardly think so, because at the end of the day people only have so much to spend, especially now we're in a recession.

I admire the example set by British toy chain The Entertainer, whose owners Gary and Cath Grant see their Christianity as central both to their business and personal lives. They give away ten per cent of all profits, choose not to open on Sundays and refuse to sell Halloween items or Harry Potter figures and books (because they encourage exploration into a darker side of life forbidden by the Scriptures). "We operate like this, not because we are successful, but because operating like this makes us successful," Gary explains.

It's time to rediscover what Joshua learnt – that prosperity and success come from honouring God and meditating on his precepts. Or as Yeshua put it in another way: "Seek first his (God's) kingdom and his righteousness, and all these (material) things will be yours as well." (From the Sermon on the Mount, Matthew 6.33)

Man-made plans are grounded

I think it appropriate at this point to include the following article I wrote for the Lifebite on-line newspaper on the eve of the 2010 British General Election:

I've been on holiday over the past week and it was an eerie experience driving around the London area in the course of visiting family. Our usually crowded skies were empty and at Heathrow Airport itself, where my brother-in-law works, the birds could be heard singing. They are normally kept well away from the runways by regular cannon fire as they have the same potential for jamming jet engines as the volcanic ash that has caused the complete shutdown of UK airspace.

The week began with the disastrous downing of the aircraft that wiped out most of Poland's leadership. And as the dark cloud that swept over Britain and beyond gathered pace, I reflected on the significance, if any, of this potentially catastrophic development.

I believe it was a week that struck at the heart of man's independence from God. There is strong speculation that the air crash was caused by the interference of impatient top brass overriding the pilot's concerns for safety, with the result that the experts were disregarded in the cause of political progress.

Meanwhile, just as the much-hyped first ever national TV election debate took place in Manchester, with the three main party leaders choosing to focus their battle on the economy, the rug was pulled from beneath them as one of the key economic factors – flight – was grounded for the first time in history. How they would rescue the economy from the disastrous recession of the past two years depended largely on 'plans' they had worked out – robbing Peter to pay Paul etc. But a natural disaster of this sort was clearly not among those plans.

The problem is that few of our politicians commit their plans to God, with the result that they are doomed to fail. In the biblical words of Solomon, "Commit to the Lord whatever you do, and your plans will succeed." And he adds, somewhat prophetically: "The Lord works out everything for his own ends – even the wicked for the day of disaster."

So as the dark, volcanic clouds gathered over the UK, it was ironic, though not surprising, that none of the questions addressed in the TV debate focused on the causes of our problems, but only on their symptoms such as the dire state of the economy and the seemingly ever-increasing spiral of crime. Instead we were given prescriptions for how the debt was going to be managed and how increased policing would do the trick. But we were completely unprepared for an Act of God – not an apparently man-made result of too much carbon emission, the reduction of which could help to save the planet. Even insurers are invoking an 'Act of God' clause to save them having to pay out £20 million in compensation. But it's taken such a dramatic event to arrest the attention of our liberal media and political elite to the fact that man does not have all the answers.

We are reminded in stark terms that no amount of man-made effort can prevent the inevitable, or ensure us of a safe and healthy future. God has the whole world in his hands – as the old gospel song says – and he will have the final say. And as the psalmist puts it, he sits in heaven and laughs at our puny efforts to put the world to rights without reference to him.

How ironic that the jet planes so maligned for punching holes in the ozone layer have all been grounded because a genuine global warming of the God kind has erupted. And it was interesting that Liberal leader Nick Clegg – an atheist – emerged the most popular in the first round of the TV debate. But I am reminded of what God told the prophet Samuel when he sent him to anoint one of Jesse's sons to be king – that God looks on the heart, not on outward appearance as man does. And none of those presented to him was God's choice. Jesse hadn't even considered David, the youngest and least thought of, who was out in the fields looking after the sheep.

Will your choice be God's choice this election? Or will it be based on outward appearance and high-sounding words? Whoever we choose, it's time to get rid of those who disregard godly values if we want to see Britain recover its greatness. "Righteousness exalts a nation, but sin is a disgrace to any people," declares the Book of Proverbs.

Nearly two years after this was written, I was encouraged by the declaration from Prime Minister David Cameron that Britain is a Christian nation which needs to return to its roots along with similar, very courageous, comments from our Queen herself.

Biblical prophecies fulfilled – Prime Minister

It was around the time of the British election that Israeli Prime Minister Binyamin Netanyahu acknowledged the authority of the Hebrew Scriptures by declaring that the prophecies of Ezekiel had been fulfilled. He did so in a stunning and remarkable moment as he participated in the 65th anniversary of the liberation of Auschwitz. Speaking to Holocaust survivors who had gathered at the notorious Auschwitz-Birkenau Nazi death camp in Poland, where more than a million Jews were murdered during World War II, Mr Netanyahu said the Holocaust represented the "dry bones" and "graves" of Ezekiel's prophecy in chapter 37 of the biblical book named after him, and that out of that horror the State of Israel was resurrected, just as the Lord said would happen.

The passage to which he referred records in part…"This is what the Sovereign Lord says: O my people, I am going to open your graves and bring you up from them; I will bring you back to the land of Israel." Ezekiel also speaks of giving them "a new heart" and "a new spirit". And quoting the biblical account of the attacks on the Jews by the people of Amalek as Moses led them out of Egypt, Mr Netanyahu urged today's Jews to "remember what Amalek did to you". Rarely has any world leader given a major address on an international stage declaring that end-time prophecies from the Bible have come true.

But there is an apparent contradiction in his understanding of God's promises, for he also told the gathering that Israel had learned that she must be prepared to defend herself. "We have learned that the only guarantee for the survival of our nation is a strong Israel and its army – the Israeli Defence Force." And he subsequently vowed as leader never again to allow the machine of evil to cut off the life of a nation that lost a third of its population on the blood-soaked earth of Europe in World War II.

Of course defence is important, but the man who has declared his trust in God's ability to fulfill his word by the way the nation was re-born in 1948 needs also to realise that God himself – and not just weaponry – is capable of protecting his people. An acknowledgement of God's intervention in the affairs of men, and especially of Israel, needs to move to complete trust. Let's pray, for example, for the Prime Minister's awareness of scriptures such as Isaiah 31.1: "Woe to those who trust in the multitude of their chariots and in the great strength of their horsemen, but do not look to the Holy One of Israel, or seek help from the Lord."

Let us also pray that he will have a growing awareness of Jesus as not just the God of the Christians, but essentially the God of the Jews – the Messiah for whom they have been waiting for millennia and of whom St Paul the Apostle said in his letter to the Christians at Ephesus: "Through him (Jesus) we both (Jews and Gentiles) have access by one Spirit to the Father."

It must be said that it was at the much-maligned 2008 meetings in Florida led by Todd Bentley – when admittedly very strange things were happening – that a prophecy was given of how God would raise up Binyamin Netanyahu to lead his people in a national revival. He has since become Prime Minister for the second time (and was recently re-elected) and shows every sign of holding out for the rights and aspirations of the Jewish people even in the face of immense pressure from their old allies – the United States.

Mr Netanyahu has shown he believes the ancient prophecies relating to the end times. He himself could be part of their fulfilment, for they also speak of spiritual revival and of the Jews having their eyes opened to the truth about their Messiah in the passages from Ezekiel already mentioned and in the Book of Zechariah who prophesies that there will come a day when God will set out to destroy all the nations that attack Jerusalem, at a time when the descendants of David – imbued with a spirit of grace and supplication – will look on the one they have pierced and bitterly mourn for him as one mourns for an only child.

I would like to conclude this chapter with the following revelation to one anonymous pastor of how Jesus is the focus of each of the 66 books of the Bible. He is the ram at Abraham's altar in Genesis, the Passover Lamb of Exodus, the High Priest of Leviticus, the cloud by day and the pillar of fire by night in the Book of Numbers, the city of our refuge in Deuteronomy and the scarlet thread out of Rahab's window in Joshua.

He is our ultimate Judge in the Book of Judges, our kinsmen-redeemer in Ruth, our trusted prophet in the two books of Samuel and our Reigning King in the books of Kings and Chronicles. He is the faithful scribe of Ezra, the re-builder of everything that is broken in Nehemiah and the Mordecai sitting faithfully at the gate in Esther.

He is our redeemer who ever lives in Job, he is our Shepherd in the Psalms, our wisdom in Proverbs and Ecclesiastes, the beautiful bridegroom of the Song of Solomon, the suffering servant of Isaiah, the weeping prophet of Jeremiah and Lamentations, the wonderful four-faced man of Ezekiel, the fourth man in the midst of Daniel's fiery furnace, our ever-faithful lover in Hosea, baptising us with the Holy Spirit in Joel, our burden bearer in Amos and our Saviour in Obadiah.

In Jonah we see him as the great foreign missionary who takes the gospel to the whole world, in Micah he is the messenger with beautiful feet, in Nahum he's the avenger, in Habakkuk the watchman who is always praying for revival, in Zephaniah the Lord mighty to save, in Haggai the restorer of our lost heritage, our fountain in Zechariah and the Son of Righteousness with healing in his wings in Malachi.

Matthew sees him as the Christ, the Son of the living God, Mark the miracle worker, Luke the Son of Man and John the door by which all must enter. In the Acts of the Apostles he's the shining light that appears to Saul on the road to Damascus, in Romans he's our justifier, in Corinthians our resurrection and sin-bearer, in Galatians he redeems us from the law, in Ephesians he's the source of our unsearchable riches, in Philippians he supplies our every need and in Colossians he is the fullness of the godhead bodily. In the letters to the Thessalonians he is our soon-coming King, in the letters to Timothy he is the mediator between God and man, in Titus he is our blessed hope and in Philemon he is a friend that sticks closer than a brother.

In the letter to the Hebrews, he is the blood of the everlasting covenant, James tells of the Lord who heals the sick and Peter paints a picture of the Chief Shepherd. John in his letters writes of the tenderness of love that comes from Jesus while Jude speaks of the Lord who is coming with thousands upon thousands of his saints and the Book of Revelation concludes by urging the church to lift up her eyes because her redemption is near, for Jesus is the King of Kings and Lord of Lords.

CHAPTER 17

Challenge to the Church

Belligerent attacks on the West in general – and Israel in particular – from Iranian president Mahmoud Ahmadinejad is just one of many biblical signs that we could soon be facing Armageddon. And the fact that Iran is soon expected to be able to produce a nuclear bomb turns what some may regard as apocalyptic fantasy into horrible reality. True, there is a growing revulsion among ordinary Iranians of the 34-year-old revolution that denies them freedom of religion and much more – and this could swing things either way, hardening the resolve of the mad dictator or ushering in a counter-revolution against the Ayatollahs. In any event, Israel fears for her existence, which has specifically been threatened by Ahmadinejad's repeated declarations to see the Jewish state "wiped off the map". And the prospect of a pre-emptive strike against Iran's nuclear facility is being seriously considered. All of which could lead to World War III.

But the Church in the West – and especially in Britain – twiddles its thumbs while the Middle East burns. You wouldn't think all of the above – which is constantly in the news – had anything whatsoever to do with Christians in general and their preachers in particular. They rarely relate current world issues to our lives and hardly ever address the specific subject of the Second Coming of Christ. In fact there is a growing move among the churches to sideline biblical prophecy altogether, and to distance 'Christianity' from any link with Israel and the Jews. This is becoming the modern heresy (which means to pick and choose what you believe rather than accept the entire 'canon' of scripture).

Well-known author and preacher Tony Campolo says that "rigid Christians" who believe in the possibility of Jesus' soon return are a real problem for the whole world, and are to blame for wars and a host of other evils. And Brian McLaren, a leader of 'the emerging church' (whatever that is) writes:

"Christians who believe Jesus Christ is coming back again are the reason there is no peace in the Middle East."

More worrying still are the remarks of best-selling author Rick Warren who appears to condemn those who study Bible prophecy – he has a huge following through his books *The Purpose-Driven Life* and *The Purpose-Driven Church*. I can only surmise that many church leaders have been so brainwashed by the politically correct mainstream media that they believe they are doing right by condemning Israel and believing that God has forsaken them. But they are sadly misled because the ancient scriptures state clearly that, even though she may have committed adultery with foreign gods, the Lord has not stopped loving her.

The despising of prophecy is useful for those who are anti-Semitic because it means they do not have to face up to the fact that God has a specific plan for Israel in the last days. But the truth is there are some 300 scriptures relating to the Second Coming in the New Testament alone (and many more in the Old), which makes it the most important subject of all. And yet so many Christians never hear it taught from their pulpits!

The message of the Second Coming is referred to in the scriptures as the 'blessed hope' because it serves to warn, encourage, comfort and bring joy in the midst of the many trials Christians were to suffer through the centuries. And though we are warned not to speculate on the precise time it would occur, we are told that the day of the Lord will come "like a thief in the night"...

"While people are saying, 'Peace and safety', destruction will come on them suddenly, as labour pains on a pregnant woman, and they will not escape."

But believers are reminded that they should not be surprised by his coming since they are not in the dark as "children of light" who should understand the signs of the times. Central to the message of the New Testament is that Jesus is a fulfilment of Old Testament prophecy, because it was this that authenticated the person of Christ, especially to Jews. The Gospel of Matthew, which has Jews specifically in mind, makes much of this.

But now we are told we mustn't look for signs as we try to understand our world from a biblical perspective, leaving Christians in ignorance of what is happening, and why. Believe me... this is devilishly devious because, if people are not looking for a fulfilment of prophecy, how will they recognise deception? You need to know that of 16 biblical prophecies relating to Israel's destiny, 13 have already been fulfilled – leaving just three to come to pass. Among those already fulfilled are their enslavement in Egypt, the possession of Canaan, their captivity in Babylon, and the worldwide scattering of Jews followed by their persecution and final re-gathering to the Promised Land. What we are still left to witness is the gathering of all nations against Jerusalem, the supernatural revelation of Christ as Messiah to the Jewish people and his final return in glory – all of which are prophesied in the (Jewish) Old Testament. The scriptures warn us not to despise prophecy – St Paul even says he would rather we prophesy than use other spiritual gifts because it builds up the church!

I will conclude by quoting from one of the greatest of Anglican bishops, J C Ryle, who was appointed in 1900 as the first Bishop of Liverpool. He said: "I believe that the Second Coming of the Lord Jesus Christ is the great event which will wind up the present dispensation, and for which we ought daily to pray." He also said: "I believe that the Jews shall ultimately be gathered again as a separate nation, restored to their own land and turned to the faith of Christ (Messiah)."

This is particularly extraordinary in view of the fact that it was not until 1948 that the Jewish nation was re-born and that Jews from all around the world began returning in droves to their ancient homeland. And many have since turned to Christ. Bishop Ryle added: "I believe that the literal sense of Old Testament prophecies has been too much neglected by the churches, and is far too much neglected at the present day, and that under the mistaken system of spiritualising and accommodating Bible language, Christians have too often missed its meaning." He further warned that Christians should not look for comfort now, but "expect their good things only after Christ's second advent."

Even President Ahmadinejad believes in the second coming – not of Christ, however, but of the Mahdi, a Muslim figure. And the Apostle James reminds us that even the demons believe – "and shudder". Believing is not enough – our faith needs to be accompanied by deeds which prove we believe, such as supporting Israel and teaching that the Second Coming of Christ is imminent.

Our spiritual forefathers encouraged Parliament to take up the cause of Israel and the need for Jews to return to the Promised Land because they saw how the Scriptures clearly indicated this outcome, but that it was incumbent upon us to play our part in bringing this about. Now that many of them are back in the land in fulfilment of ancient prophecies, we still have a duty to defend their cause, particularly since they are being hounded and harassed from all sides. Church leaders should not be adding fuel to the fire of antagonism against Israel by peddling lies designed to stir up hatred. Rather they should be at the forefront of influencing media and politicians who are generally so misinformed and ignorant about this very complex issue. Clergymen also need to get off the fence and help their congregations rediscover the Hebraic roots of their faith, and that the church has not replaced the Jews as the apple of God's eye but has in fact been 'grafted in to the Olive Tree' from which salvation – and the Messiah – has come. The Jews have not been rejected by God (Jeremiah 31.37, Romans 11.1) but Gentile followers of Jesus the

Jew share the nourishing sap from the olive root (Rom 1.17). "You do not support the root, but the root supports you…" the Jewish apostle Paul reminded the early Roman Christians (v18). If God had rejected them, he would reject you too (v23). Their national rejection is only temporary, for one day all Israel will be saved (v26) "for God's gifts and his call are irrevocable" (v29). And we are called to play our part for, as Jesus said, "Whatever you did for one of the least of these brothers of mine, you did for me." (Matthew 25)

I conclude with the challenge I made at the beginning: If you love Jesus, you will love the Jew.

World chaos: it's all about Israel!

I began this book with an overall review of Israel's place in God's plans, originally written in May 2008 for the 60th anniversary of the modern state. Nearly five years down the line we in Britain are in the midst of a grave economic crisis with a social structure literally falling apart. All the nations – especially in the West – are being shaken to their very foundations and the whole world is in turmoil, not only with economies collapsing but also with natural disasters adding to the despair. What in the world is happening?

I have already outlined the reasons why that tiny, beleaguered nation is so much the focus of world attention. And now there are many theological and other pundits who see the state of the global finances as a divine judgment on the nations for the way in which they are trying to divide the land God promised the Jews 4,000 years ago. Not content with denying Israel even a fraction of the territory Britain and her allies, and even the League of Nations (the predecessor of the UN), had promised them, they have been ganging up like bullies in a bid to push the fledging nation into a corner. But land now considered 'occupied' belongs to the Jew by right – politically speaking as well as by divine command. How much more kosher can you get?

Yet modern politicians – mere men – seek to write off God's word as null and void. And for this they are under judgment – for the Jews are God's chosen people from ancient times, the 'apple of his eye'. Now we are facing a possible nuclear conflict the like of which the world has never seen, though prophesied in the Bible as an end-time scenario. Iran, implacably opposed to Israel, is building nuclear weapons with the intention of 'wiping them off the map' while the terrorists they sponsor – Hamas and Hezbollah – prefer to 'drive them into the sea'.

And yet some of our political masters believe the lie that Hamas and the Palestinians are the victims while the Israelis are the bullies – reversing the position in which Jews have found themselves over the centuries: butchered, bloodied and crushed under foot. Too many have forgotten the Holocaust too soon and are prepared to contribute to another by backing Iranian-supported terrorists who want to destroy the only democracy in the Middle East while Israel can no longer rely on American support in the face of growing hostility from President Obama which leaves them more vulnerable than ever.

It is not surprising that we in the West are in such peril – with economies collapsing, rioting in the streets, atmospheric plagues grounding air space, the sea being polluted by oil and families breaking up as never before under pressure from our 'do as you please' society. British preacher Lance Lambert, a highly regarded prophet of our times who now lives in Israel, has predicted these events. Way back in 1986, he delivered a message on Mount Carmel that "unparalleled upheaval and turmoil" would soon come upon the world including terrorism, monetary collapses and natural disasters. He predicted that the power of Communism would be broken (that happened three years later) and that Islam would be next.

In his prophecy, he said Jesus had never forgotten the Jewish people – he was still their King, although unnoticed by many of them. "There was no gas chamber, no massacre in which I was not present, but now the time has surely come when I shall receive them, for I will reveal myself to them and, with astonishment, they will recognise me." This refers to the time, to which I have already alluded, when the Jews would finally recognise "the one they have pierced" and mourn for him as one would for an only son.

In a further prophecy given in 1992, Lambert said the Lord would cause political, economic, religious and physical upheavals and warned of an emerging 'New World Order' which would be like Babylon of old – the spirit of antichrist – seeking to unite the world without him. He added that the Lord would judge every nation and leader that opposed his purpose.

In 1998, at a conference in the Philippines, he said that because the nations were dividing his land and seeking to destroy his heritage, God would judge them "with natural disasters, by physical catastrophes, by fire, by flood, by earthquake and by eruptions", adding: "I will touch the seas, the atmosphere, the earth and all that is within them. Moreover, I will touch them where it will hurt them most; for I will touch their power and the foundations of their affluence and prosperity. I will smash their prosperous economies, says the Lord. They sit like potentates, so safe, so secure, believing in their own cleverness and wisdom and power; but I, the Lord, will cause them to stumble. I will lead them into confusion and disorder. I will blind them and delude them so that they will make mistakes because they have not regarded me, nor honoured me; but rather they have devalued me, deriding my word and ignoring my covenants."

. in the eye of the storm, Israel will recognise their Messiah and her ⟨?⟩ will be restored. In a 2006 message Lambert pointed out that those ⟨?⟩ions – like the UK – who had become great and powerful through God's ⟨?⟩ace but who were now rejecting him would be judged with particular ⟨?⟩arshness. And in a more recent message delivered in 2010 he warns of a far more serious phase of judgment on nations opposed to his purpose for Israel in which old and powerful nations would become like third world countries. Amidst all the shaking, he said, two peoples lie at its heart – Israel, and the living church. "I will use these matters, these events, to purify one and to save the other."

ISRAEL
THE CHOSEN

Why the Jews are so special

Charles Gardner